Tallinn

the Bradt City Guide

Neil Taylor

edition

2

www.bradtguides.com

Bradt Travel Guides Ltd, UK
The Globe Pequot Press Inc, USA

Detail on House of Blackheads (JS) page 93

PAGARIÄRI

Café on Suur-Karja, Old Town (FH) page 85

Tallinn's Old Town (FD/Tips)

KUNOMITEHINDA

ÕMBLUS-
ATELJEE

Town Hall Square (LR) page 111

Ice sculpture, Snelli Park (FH)

Raekoja Street, behind the Town Hall (ES)

Piiskopi Street and Alexander Nevsky Cathedral (M) page 150

Clock on the Holy Ghost Church (CN) page 152

Jugenstil sculpture on the Russian Embassy (CN)

Old Town as seen from the harbour (FD/Tips)

Author

Neil Taylor was from 1975 to 2005 Director of Regent Holidays, a British tour company that has specialised in travel to the Baltic states and Kaliningrad since 1991. He visits the area about four times a year and in 1999 his Bradt guide to Estonia was first published. It is now in its fourth edition. He is on the Board of the Association of Independent Tour Operators (AITO) and writes and broadcasts on general travel trade topics. In 2000, Neil was awarded the Lifetime Achievement Award by the British Guild of Travel Writers, of which he is now also a member.

FEEDBACK REQUEST

It doesn't matter how often I visit Tallinn: every time I go there, there is something new to entice the visitor. If you would like to share your comments about places I have mentioned in the guide, or tell me about something new that you have discovered, please do drop me a line at neiltaylor90@hotmail.com, or c/o Bradt Travel Guides, 23 High Street, Chalfont St Peter, Bucks SL9 9QE.

Second edition published January 2007
First published 2004

Bradt Travel Guides Ltd
23 High Street, Chalfont St Peter, Bucks SL9 9QE, England
Published in the US by The Globe Pequot Press Inc, 246 Goose Lane, PO Box 480,
Guilford, Connecticut 06437-0480

A catalogue record for this book is available from the British Library

ISBN-10: 1 84162 179 X   ISBN-13: 978 1 84162 179 1

Photographers Jon Arnold Images/Alamy (JA), Focus Database/Tips (FD), Fran Hallett (FH), Tricia Hayne
(TH), Christian Nowak (CN), Luis Rosa (LR), Jonathan Smith (JS), Esko Syvänen (ES), Joanna Vaughn (JV)
Cover Old Town from Toompea (JA)
Title page Alexander Nevsky Cathedral (JS), House of Blackheads (JS)

Maps Steve Munns   **Illustrations** Carole Vincer, Dave Colton

Typeset from the author's disk by Wakewing   Printed and bound in Spain by Grafo SA, Bilbao

Contents

Acknowledgements   VI

Introduction   VII

How to Use this Book   IX

1 **Contexts**   1
History 1, Politics 9, Economy 11, People 14, Local charities 15,
Business 16, Religion 16, Culture and festivals 17, Public holidays 18,
Geography and climate 18

2 **Planning**   21
The city – a practical overview 21, When to visit 23, Suggested
itineraries 24, Tour operators 26, Red tape 28, Estonian embassies
overseas 29, Getting there and away 30, Health 34, Safety 35, What to
take 35, Money and budgeting 38

3 **Practicalities**   **40**
Banks and credit cards 40, Local media 42, Communications 42,
Embassies 45, Hospitals and pharmacies 46, Religious services 46,
Tourist information 47

4 **Local Transport**   **49**
Tallinn airport 49, Taxis 50, Local buses/trams and trolleybuses 51, Car
hire 52, Cycling 52

5 **Accommodation**   **54**
Prices 55, Luxury 56, First class 58, Tourist class 65

6 **Eating and Drinking**   **74**
Prices 75, Restaurants 76, Cafés and bars 85

7 **Entertainment and Nightlife**   **92**
Opera, concerts and cinema 93, Nightlife 94, Gay Tallinn 97

8 **Shopping**   **99**
Books and postcards 99, Souvenirs 101, Food and drink 104

9   **Walking Tours**   **106**
Walk one 106, Further walks 115

10   **What to See and Do**   **123**
Museums 123, Churches 150, Parks and gardens 156

11   **Beyond the City**   **157**
Rocca al Mare Open Air Museum 157, Paldiski 159,
Around Tallinn Bay 162, Naissaar 173, Lahemaa National Park 176,
Day trip to Helsinki 187

12   **Language**   **194**
Pronunciation 194, Useful words and expressions 196

13   **Further Information**   **203**
Books 203, Maps 205, Websites 205

Index   **209**

Acknowledgements

All foreign writers on Estonia begin their research at the Estonian Institute, either at its offices or via the website. Their help in both ways is invaluable and the good-humoured nature of their publications must persuade many first-time readers to deepen their interest in the country. The National Heritage Board lobbies hard for conservation and preservation. Anneli Randla and Kaire Tooming are always very generous with their time whenever I am in Tallinn and both have tracked down much useful material for me.

The Tallinn Tourist Board leapt into activity as soon as Estonia became independent and it has kept up the pace ever since. I am always grateful for the help that Helena Tsistova and Tiina Kiibus give me in my constant struggle to keep up to date in such a rapidly changing city.

At Bradt, it would be invidious to mention any one member of staff; my haphazard style of work creates havoc for them all but I am immensely grateful for their tolerance and good humour and of course for their worldwide efforts in promoting my books.

Introduction

Whether approached by air, land or sea, Tallinn is immediately identifiable as a capital that looks west rather than east. The departure board at the airport lists London, Copenhagen and Stockholm but rarely St Petersburg. The boats that fill the harbour, be they massive ferries or small yachts, head for Finland and Sweden, not Russia. The traffic jams that are beginning to block the main streets are caused by Volkswagens, Land Rovers and Saabs, not by Ladas. Links with the West are celebrated, those with Russia are commemorated. In May 1998, Tallinn celebrated its 750th anniversary since on 15 May 1248 it adopted Lübeck Town Law, which united most members of the Hanseatic League. A month later, as on every 14 June, flags were lowered in memory of those deported to the Soviet Union on 14 June 1941. In May 2005, the Estonian president turned down an invitation to visit Moscow to 'celebrate' the 60th anniversary of the Soviet victory over Germany.

Immediately after independence Western goods started pouring into the shops, and Russian ones are now very hard to find. There is a similar reluctance to buy from any of the other former Soviet republics, even wine from Georgia or brandy from Armenia. Architecturally, with the exception of the Alexander Nevsky Cathedral, it is the Germans, Swedes and Danes who have left their imposing mark on the churches and fortifications of the Old Town. Tallinn was always ready to defend itself but in the end never did so. It has suffered many occupations but, apart from a Soviet bombing raid in 1944, the city has not been physically harmed as no battles were ever fought there.

The division in Tallinn between what is now the Old Town on the hill (Toompea) and the newer town around the port has survived political administrations of every hue. It has divided God from Mammon, Tsarist and Soviet governors from their reluctant Estonian subjects, and now the Estonian parliament from successful bankers, merchants and manufacturers who thrive on whatever coalition happens to be in power. Tallinn has no Capitol Hill or Whitehall. The parliament building is one of the most modest in the Old Town, dwarfed by the town walls and surrounding churches. When fully restored, the Old Town will be an outstanding permanent monument to Gothic and Baroque architecture, and a suitable backcloth to formal political and religious activity. Outside its formidable walls, contemporary Tallinn is changing rapidly according to the demands of the new business ethos. Travellers who arrived by boat in the early 1990s just saw one Tallinn as they approached the harbour, the Old Town with a skyline that had not changed since the 1890s when the Russian cathedral was built. Travellers coming in 2007 have two distinct views – the Old Town as before, but an increasing number of skyscrapers around the harbour, representing for the first time in 800 years a truly Estonian stamp on Tallinn. Travellers coming in 2008 are likely to be welcomed by a 30-metre tall statue rising out of the water in the harbour, Tallinn's answer to Berlin's Molecule Man. It will represent Kalevipoeg, Estonia's mythical hero whose talents included walking on water.

How to Use this Book

HOTEL PRICES These always fluctuate wildly according to the booking agency used, the time of year and the day of the week. Take those listed only as a rough indication and, with the number of hotels due to open in Tallinn during 2007, expect some reductions.

RESTAURANT PRICES These always include VAT but rarely service; adding 10% for this is normal practice. Fixed-price lunches are beginning to be offered but this is still not common in Tallinn and prices are usually the same for lunch and for dinner.

OPENING HOURS Not many cafés open for breakfast as hotels include it in their room rates and Estonians live close enough to work to be able to eat at home. Once open from 10.00 or so, cafés divide into those which close around 17.00 and those likely still to be open at midnight. Restaurants open at 12.00 and do not usually close during the afternoon. Their closing times vary enormously so if you want to eat late, you will certainly have a choice, but check the closing time if you have a particular favourite. Restaurants open seven days a week throughout the year and, much as they would like to pretend otherwise, bookings in advance are rarely necessary.

Most museums close at least one day a week, some for two days. Usually this is a Monday or Tuesday. They open around 10.30–11.00 and close around 17.00–18.00. Policies vary around national holidays so do check beforehand at those times. Pre-booked groups can usually arrange for museums to be opened specially for them.

EMAIL ADDRESSES Where one is given, assume that correspondence in English is fine.

WEBSITES In this book it can normally be assumed that if a website address is given, it has an English text. Many restaurants publish their menus on their sites.

MAP REFERENCES (eg: [2 G1]) relate to the colour map section at the end of the guide.

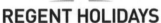

TALLINN AT A GLANCE

Location Estonia is the most northerly of the Baltic states, bordering Latvia to the south and Russia to the north and east. Tallinn is on the Gulf of Finland, 80km from Helsinki. Flights from London take about 3 hours; from Helsinki by helicopter about 20 minutes. Boats to Helsinki take 2–3 hours; bus to Riga about 5 hours.

Population 380,000

Language Estonian

Religion Amongst the small number of Estonians who profess a religion, the Lutheran and Orthodox faiths predominate.

Time GMT/BST +2 hours (as neighbouring Baltic states)

International telephone code +372

Currency Estonian kroon (EEK); € 1 = 15.65EEK

Electricity 220v; two-pin plugs

Public holidays 1 January, 24 February, 23–24 June, 20 August, 25 December

School holidays Mid June to 1 September; short breaks at Christmas and Easter

Climate Daytime temperatures November–February around 0°C, March–May, September–October, 10–20°C; June–August 20–25°C

1 Contexts

HISTORY

Written records on Tallinn date only from the 12th century although it is clear that a small port existed much earlier. When recent archaeological discoveries are fully analysed, they will probably show evidence of the Estonians as conquerors before then, rather than as the victims they were to become for the next 800 years. The failure of Tallinn to develop as a port earlier was probably due to rampant piracy on the water and poor agriculture inland. In 1219, the Danes occupied Tallinn and much of what is now northern Estonia, on the pretext of spreading Christianity. The name Tallinn dates from this time and in Estonian actually means 'Danish city'. Although this name was chosen to suggest only temporary occupation, it has been maintained. The first German merchants settled in 1228 and they were to maintain their economic domination until 1939, even during the long periods of Swedish and Tsarist rule. Their elaborate coats of arms, displayed in the Dome and Niguliste churches, were a formal expression of this power. When, for instance, the Swedes surrendered to the Russians in 1710, the capitulation documents confirmed that German would remain the official language of commerce. 1343 would be the last time before 1917 that Estonians attempted to overthrow their

TALLINN BEFORE WORLD WAR II

From 'Keepers of the Baltic Gates' by John Gibbons, written in autumn 1938
Tallinn fascinated me; it is like plenty of other cities with an old part on top of a hill and a new part down below. If that was all I had wanted, I need have gone no further from London than Lincoln. But it was the general atmosphere and the people which so struck me. Here was none of the wealthy prosperity of Stockholm nor the studied modernity of Helsinki. Instead I was seeing a melange that I had met nowhere else with a ferocious grasp at gaiety that was as far removed from the natural happiness of Latindom as from the unbending stolidity of Saxonhood and Scandinavia.

On top of the Tallinn hill, I was in a quarter that might almost have been an English cathedral close. The nobility used to live there, but now it houses government ministries whose gentlemen staff might almost have been English themselves, so perfectly do they speak our tongue. Up and down all Estonia there are plenty of similar gentlemen politely eager to show their hospitality to the stranger and to make a guest welcome to their land.

occupiers. Reval, the German name for Tallinn, is sometimes seen in English publications; it probably comes from *Revala*, the old Estonian name for the surrounding area. A more colourful explanation is that it comes from the two German words *Reh* and *Fall*, meaning the falling of the deer as they attempt to escape the Danish occupation.

Coming downhill again, the streets were not the decorous promenades of cultured Finland. Here and there will be a chattering group of girls in what they think are the latest fashions of the Western world and then there could be a couple of old men in huge shabby coats that were probably first worn in Russian days now 20 years past. Everywhere there were students. In a land as new as prairie Canada one rather wonders how on earth they are going to find employment for all these anxious scholars.

By accident I found myself at what the guidebook calls the 'unimpressive Swedish Church of St Michael'. The architecture was indeed unimpressive – I only recall a lot of whitewash – but the congregation was the reverse. These people were so terribly and so wholeheartedly earnest. As the preacher droned on, even I of an alien creed could appreciate their attentiveness. There was no apparent oratory, no gestures, no ritual, nothing but the Word of God and they were following every word with an almost fierce eagerness. There is nothing indifferentist about Estonia.

Peter the Great visited Tallinn on 11 different occasions, so crucial was the city as an ice-free port to his empire. In 1711, he joined Christmas celebrations in Town Hall Square. He instigated the permanent expansion of Tallinn beyond the city walls by building Kadriorg Palace near the coast about two miles from the Old Town. The previous history of constant warfare at least in the vicinity of the town had led to all

3

A DESCRIPTON OF TALLINN IN 1984

Kate Wharton

I spent last week in one of the saddest cities in the world, Tallinn in Estonia, famed for its medieval and 18th-century architecture. Extraordinarily, this tiny backwater of the Soviet Empire has been in the news recently as its people were warned by the voice of *Pravda*, Moscow's main daily newspaper at the time, that they were not Soviet enough. Suddenly the secrets of this benighted land began to emerge. So, last week, determined to find out about the real Estonia, I became the first Western journalist in the country for many, many months, and certainly the first since Estonia came back into the news.

At issue in Estonia is the enforced Russification of their land and the disappearance of their language and all their customs. The blue, black and white flag of independent Estonia

buildings being makeshift wooden houses which could easily be burnt as a preliminary defence to the city. Tallinn was then to enjoy 200 years of peace and increasing prosperity. Architecturally, though, the Old Town has always remained the centre of Tallinn and its main attraction. Gert Walter, a Baltic German who settled in East Germany and could therefore return to Tallinn during the Soviet period, describes the Old Town as having half a per cent of the surface area of Tallinn but giving it its entire magic.

was banished in 1944. Today the Russian flag is everywhere. So is the huge figure of 40, accompanied by a hammer and sickle, to remind everyone that the yoke has been in place for 40 years and is intended to be there in excess of 40 x 40. Already more than half the population, 52%, is Russian rather than Estonian and by 1987, when the vast military harbour outside Tallinn is finished, the proportion will rise to 65%.

About 65,000 Estonians fled to the West in 1944. Thousands more were deported to remote parts of the Soviet Union and most of the present-day dissidents now rot in Russian labour camps. As Ernst Jaakson, Estonian Consul-General in New York, told me: 'There is hardly an Estonian family in existence that has not been separated from its loved ones or nearest relatives as a result of the Soviet occupation.'
Published in 'The Mail on Sunday', 2 September 1984

The completion of the railway link with St Petersburg in 1870 turned Tallinn into a major city. The port was enlarged to handle the increasing volume of goods that could now be brought there and factories were established to take advantage of the larger markets. In the 20th century, most events that would determine Estonia's future took place in Tallinn. Independence was declared there in 1918 and in 1991, German occupations were imposed there also in 1918 and again in 1941. The Soviets came in 1940 and then chased the Germans out in 1944. In the 20th century, the Russians and Germans between them occupied Tallinn seven times, and the country has been independent three times, although it has to be admitted that independence on the first occasion in 1918 lasted only for one day. Britain can claim considerable credit for ensuring that the next period of independence would last much longer – 20 years. Intervention by the Royal Navy during 1918–19 in the Gulf of Finland near Tallinn ensured that neither the Bolsheviks nor the Germans were able to conquer Estonia at that time.

The port always adapted to the political circumstances in which it found itself. During the first independence period from 1920 to 1940 it exported large quantities of timber and dairy products to Britain as the market to the new Soviet Union was lost. Passenger services linked it with all its Baltic neighbours. It would suffer a moribund 45 years from 1945 until 1990 with little international trade being allowed. However it did have one crucial link to the West, denied to Riga in Latvia and Klaipeda in Lithuania. A twice-weekly ferry service operated for Finnish visitors from the 1960s; its effect was psychological rather than practical given that very few Estonians indeed were allowed to use it in Soviet times. It did at least allow Tallinn to feel it was not totally cut off from its European past and that it might again sometime have a European future. This service rapidly increased to a boat an hour during the 1990s as the notorious 'vodka tourists' poured in, together with some other visitors who had broader interests. Whilst 2.5 million passengers a year come to Tallinn on this route, the port has to battle hard with Russian, Latvian and Lithuanian ports for the transit traffic in goods from Russia and central Asia.

Between 1945 and 1990 the city's population doubled in size to 500,000, about 30% of the total population of Estonia. Since then, Tallinn's population, like that of the whole country, has dropped considerably as couples delay starting families and living on one's own becomes more popular. It is now (2006) around 380,000. The year 2002 was the first year since 1990 when more births than deaths were registered.

DATES IN THE HISTORY OF TALLINN

1219 Danish forces under Waldemar II occupy Tallinn

1248 Tallinn joins Hanseatic League

1343 St George's Night Rebellion on 14 May

1346 Denmark sells Tallinn to the Teutonic Knights

1372 German replaces Latin as the official language

1422 Opening of Town Hall pharmacy, which still operates from the same site

1492 St Nicholas' Church receives its first legacy of silver

1524 First Lutheran sermon preached in Tallinn – at St Olav's

1535 The first catechism is published in Estonian

1561 Swedes occupy Tallinn

1591 5,000 people, about half the population, die from the plague

1633 First British trading company, Thomas Clayhills, opens

1684 Much of Old Town destroyed in a fire

1710 Russian army under Peter the Great seizes Tallinn

1772 Tallinn's first newspaper is published, in German

1790 Swedish navy fails to seize Tallinn from the Russians

1820 Census gives population as 13,000 with 5,500 Germans, 4,400 Estonians and 2,300 Russians

1854 British and French blockade harbour during Crimean War

1870 Railway to St Petersburg opened

1887 Russian replaces German as the language of instruction in all schools

1905 Frequent protests and strikes against Tsarist regime

1908 Tsar Nicholas II and King Edward VII meet on their yachts in Tallinn harbour

1910 Statue of Peter the Great erected celebrating 200 continuous years of Tsarist rule

1917 Bolsheviks seize Tallinn from Germans

1918 Estonian independence declared on 24 February

1919 Royal Navy establishes base on Naissaar Island in Tallinn harbour

1920 Tartu Peace Treaty in February brings war with USSR to an end

1924 An attempted coup by 300 armed communists is crushed on 1 December

1928 Performance of first Estonian opera

1931 First 'Miss Estonia' contest held

1937 First of two British-built submarines delivered in Tallinn harbour to the Estonian navy

1938 Tallinn census gives population as 146,000 and notes 17 hotels and 25 foreign legations in the town. Extensive celebrations mark the 20th anniversary of Estonian independence

1939 Baltic-German families all forced to 'return home' to Germany
1940 Soviet forces occupy Tallinn on 16 June
1941 German forces occupy Tallinn on 28 August
1944 Soviet forces reoccupy Tallinn on 22 September
1950 Population of Tallinn reaches 200,000
1955 First television programmes transmitted in Estonian
1965 Twice-weekly ferry service opens to Helsinki and for 25 years will be its only link abroad
1980 Olympic Games sailing events held in Tallinn
1989 Estonian flag is raised on Tall Hermann Tower on 24 February
1991 Estonian government formed in Tallinn
1994 Last Russian troops leave Tallinn
2002 Eurovision Song Contest held in Tallinn
2004 Estonia joins the EU on 1 May
2006 Lennart Meri, president 1992–2000, dies on 13 March
     Queen Elizabeth II visits Tallinn, 19–20 October

POLITICS

Estonia nationally and Tallinn locally has been governed since independence in 1991 by a rapidly changing series of coalitions. Yet these are hardly noticed outside the country as few policy disputes impinge on foreign tourists or business visitors. Some mayors, emulating Jacques Chirac in Paris or Willy Brandt in Berlin, have used the position as an entrée into national politics. Others have followed Ken Livingstone in London to use it as an alternative power base. Edgar Savisaar, mayor from 2001 to 2004 has been the most famous person in this position. He was Estonia's first prime minister in 1991–92 having played a prominent role in the run-up to independence. Currently (October 2006) he is minister of economics and was a close supporter of President Arnold Rüütel, whose attempt in September 2006 to be re-elected for a second term failed. This is likely to be only a temporary setback to his national ambitions. He attracts intense support and total contempt in equal quantity. His opponents call him the 'rhinoceros' given his toughness and unwillingness to compromise. The articles that fill the local papers would have a familiar ring to residents in any large western European city, were they able to read them. Accusations of incompetence, of personal greed and of corruption are the regular fare. The few parts of Old Tallinn with roads wide enough for cars tried a congestion charge but then gave it up. It took at least a year to decide how much space under a major square a car park and a bus station should have between them. Funds and programmes for drug rehabilitation on the 'sink' estates are always inadequate.

Jüri Ratas, the mayor elected in November 2005, quickly took the environment as his major commitment to the city. A visit to Lyon in France convinced him of the need to make serious provision for cyclists; dedicated lanes on all major roads and properly guarded parking lots followed in 2006. He would like Tallinn to be a seriously green city in time for its 2011 accolade as the European Capital of Culture, but admits this will most likely have to be achieved over a much longer timescale. Tallinn may well gain a higher international profile in the future due to the defeat of the very inward-looking President Arnold Rüütel by Toomas Henrik Ilves, who is renowned for his more international outlook, in the September 2006 presidential elections.

If tourists are coming to Tallinn from all over the world, the residents can hardly yet be called cosmopolitan. Roughly 60% are ethnically Estonian and the other 40% Russian. They hardly mix and few Russians are in senior jobs. With any Estonian over 30 still having bitter memories of Soviet times, it is not surprising that no signs are in Russian, that the public sector works exclusively in Estonian and that some knowledge of Estonian is a requirement for citizenship. Russians unable or unwilling to learn Estonian are doomed to endure the jobs that in other countries are imposed on immigrants; in other words, work that locals can always avoid for something better paid and more comfortable. All ethnic Estonians were saddened by the death in March 2006 of their first president Lennart Meri who had so skilfully led them into independence.

ECONOMY

Unlike other former Soviet republics, Estonia never had any doubts about plunging immediately into a capitalist economy and it established a tax system which encouraged extensive foreign investment. The public sector withdrew from agriculture and industry and to some extent also from transport. Visitors who travel to the suburbs will notice competitive bus companies operating on similar routes. The

Michael Bourdeaux

For 15 years after World War II, Tallinn was a closed city, nestling amongst the forest of defensive (offensive) weaponry trained on the NATO countries. Suddenly in 1960 it was opened to Western visitors. I was lucky enough to have been a student at Moscow University at the time, so in May 1960 I was perhaps the first British visitor. I not only went there by train from Leningrad but also stayed illegally in a private house for the first and only time during the 25 years that I knew the Soviet Union. Far from being worried that I would bring trouble on their heads, the occupants barred the exit and refused to let me out until I had agreed to stay for three nights, having found my photograph displayed on their wall!

All of us, as if by common agreement, steered clear of the topic of the Soviet occupation but the family thoroughly organised my time for the next three days. After eight months in drab winter Moscow, the élan of ancient Tallinn in its bright spring colours took me into a new world. A visit on Sunday to Kaide's Lutheran church,

kroon instantly replaced the Russian rouble in 1992, whereas in the two neighbouring Baltic countries transitional currencies were maintained for another year. The kroon was tied to the German mark and has kept to the same peg with the euro. Value added tax was not only introduced but was collected too. Worries as the country entered the

Charles's Church, left mixed impressions. Strangely, the family did not want to accompany me. This huge church was about half full, with 40% of the congregation younger people, a far higher proportion than one saw in Russia. I tried to see the pastor after the service, but the corridor was blocked by dozens of young people waiting outside his door. None of these, to my surprise, would speak to me, although most must have known Russian. I surmised they were waiting for religious instruction, illegal under the Soviet system at the time, and were unwilling for a foreigner (or a Russian if they took me for one) to intrude.

On my final day, having purchased an air ticket to Riga, I was waiting on the tarmac beside a small aeroplane. An official came up to me, demanded my documents, took me inside and told me my intended flight was illegal for a foreigner. 'Our rules are less strict than yours in Britain for Soviet citizens,' he said. 'When I was there, I was prevented from visiting many places. You can go where you like, but not always by your chosen route. Visit Riga by all means, but you must do so by train via Leningrad.'

EU centred on the role that Finland and Sweden might play in the economy as manufacturing, distribution and land ownership slipped from Estonian hands. It was originally planned that Estonia would join the euro in 2007 but inflation in 2005–06 caused largely by increased fuel prices is delaying this until at least 2008.

PEOPLE

Nothing hurts Estonians more than to be called Russians or Balts. They have minimal interest in either Russia or Latvia and their language is closer to that of the Finns. They are not interested in small talk, preferring to get to the point quickly. In business, they are not aggressive, feeling that a calmer approach is more likely to get results. In print, they are more serious than British writers tend to be, so do not expect any caustic asides or irony in the locally produced guidebooks or histories. (Those produced by the Estonian Institute are a welcome exception.) As most families lost several members to the Siberian prison camps in the 1941 and 1949 deportations, it is not surprising that many still feel resentful towards any Russian they meet.

THE LOCAL COMMUNITY Tallinn is rigidly divided between the 60% of the population who speak Estonian and the 40% who speak Russian. Seeing so little written in Russian, it is hard to believe that they form such a large percentage of the population. This virtual ban on its use is an understandable reaction to 50 years of Soviet occupation. The Russians are largely restricted to menial jobs that Estonians no longer wish to do. Expect to find them as chambermaids, shop assistants and waiters but not in offices or at the reception desks of grand hotels. Russians who want to get on in Tallinn learn Estonian as quickly as possible and try to put their past behind them.

Estonians do not react in any special way when dealing with foreigners. So many have relatives abroad, and/or have now left the country themselves for holidays or to work, that they speak English, see English-speaking films and have no problem in relating to outsiders. In fact, absorbing Western food and brand names and indulging in the consumer culture is a further mechanism for distancing themselves from the Soviet past and the Russian present. The future must see some form of reconciliation towards the Russians, perhaps similar to that which came about in France, Belgium and Holland towards the Germans in the 1960s as a new generation grows up with no memories of the occupation. Business to some extent demands this as Estonia has to sell itself as a transit route for goods from Russia. Tallinn is also promoting itself there as a tourist destination, whilst there are still older people nostalgic for the holidays they spent in Tallinn in Soviet times. On the other hand, EU membership since 2004 has increased the divisions between Estonia and its former master.

LOCAL CHARITIES

The culture of volunteering has yet to catch on in Estonia. Perhaps as one of the few Soviet legacies still remaining, the state continues to be seen as responsible for any initiative in the public sector. It is therefore very difficult to generate community interest in say improvements for a school or church. In the immediate aftermath of independence, the Estonian community abroad funded many projects in the public sector, as did the EU. Although many Estonians at home could now take this on, they do not do so. Perhaps those who see how active volunteers are elsewhere will start to generate similar behaviour in Estonia.

BUSINESS

Most foreigners are pleasantly surprised by the directness of the Estonian approach to business. They will want to establish quickly whether there is common ground and they do not waste time on small talk; in other words, the approach is the complete opposite of that used in many Asian countries. They are happy to talk shop over a light lunch but will not expect glamorous evenings to be part of the negotiating pattern. For business purposes, there is no need to waste time trying to learn a few words of Estonian. These will probably be misunderstood anyway as so few foreigners can speak the language with a remotely acceptable accent. English is the normal language of business with foreigners and even between Estonians and ethnic Russians as some Estonians are very reluctant to admit to knowing Russian.

RELIGION

As the Church had a somewhat underground role in the Soviet period, it is difficult to give a clear picture of religious allegiance, both then and in contemporary Estonia. A few Lutheran and Orthodox churches continued to function after 1945 but many were converted to other uses and there was no religious education in schools. Most reopened again either during the perestroika era or after the restoration of independence, but funding remains a great problem. Of the 20% of the population who profess to religious convictions, about half are Lutheran and half Orthodox. The Orthodox community is divided into the Estonian and the Russian. Tallinn, unlike Riga or Vilnius, never had a large Jewish community and so was spared the worst brutality of the Holocaust.

CULTURE AND FESTIVALS

With the three Baltic states, it is normally easier to say what divides them rather than what unites them. However, a passion for choral singing, initially started as a protest movement against Tsarist rule, was continued during the first period of independence (1918–40) and shows no signs of abating now. The Song Festival which takes place every four years in Tallinn used to be a barometer of Soviet control. Political analysts observed every word, every gesture and the colours of the performers' clothes. Blue, black and white represented the banned national flag. Now it reflects a genuine commitment to music. The Song Festival in summer 2004 hosted over 20,000 participants and 250,000 visitors.

The summer of 2006 saw the start of regular musical performances on Naissaar Island, for which the audience is taken by boat from Pirita and then brought back at the end of the evening. Costs were around 500EEK for the boat and ticket combined. This is likely to be continued and extended during 2007. The website www.nargenopera.ee will have full information.

For most of the year, tourists in Tallinn can be sure their visit will coincide with an annual music festival. Organ music, jazz and dancing are regular features and Estonian pop singers now compete with famous names from abroad for loyal audiences at the Saku Suurhall, venue of the 2002 Eurovision Song Contest. As Tallinn hotels are full during the peak summer months, more and more festivals are arranged at other times of year. Before booking a holiday, visitors should check the Tallinn Tourist Board website (*www.tourism.tallinn.ee*) to see what is on when they plan to go, and perhaps consider changing their dates.

PUBLIC HOLIDAYS

New Year's Day	1 January
Independence Day	24 February
Midsummer	23–4 June
Restoration of Independence Day	20 August
Christmas Day	25 December

GEOGRAPHY AND CLIMATE

Tallinn, with the Old Town based around a hillside, gives a misleading impression of Estonia as a whole. The rest of the town and the rest of the country are very flat indeed. The highest point in Estonia is just 300m above sea level. It is a hill near the Latvian border which is referred to locally as a mountain, since by comparison with the rest of the country, it represents such a protruding landmark. Tallinn is situated on a bay which contains several islands. Two of these, Aegna and Naissaar, had thriving fishing communities until World War II, then became secret Soviet bases and are now reinventing themselves as nature reserves.

CLIMATE Tallinn is fortunate that it is reached by the Gulf Stream. Whilst for much of the winter temperatures do fall below freezing, days when they fall below –10°C are few and far between. There is usually one bitterly cold spell each winter when temperatures fall for two to three days down to –20°C. January 2006 had a particularly cold start when they dropped to –25°C. Global warming has of course tended to make the winters milder, so whilst icebreakers are still needed to keep the harbour open, they are no longer in daily use. Spring and autumn are short seasons in Estonia, with winter weather common from mid October until April. From March to May and September to October, expect temperatures of 10–20°C in the daytime. Summer can be said to start in mid May and continue until mid September. The weather is changeable throughout the summer, with bright sunshine often turning suddenly to rain within an hour or so. Temperatures are pleasantly mild in comparison with those around the Mediterranean at that time, unlikely to drop below 15°C. The norm is 20–25°C, with heatwaves – up to 30°C – being rare.

Current weather in Tallinn and forecasts for the next few days can be checked on www.weather.ee/tallinn.

2 Planning

THE CITY – A PRACTICAL OVERVIEW

Tallinn has an ideal layout for the short-break visitor. Many tourists will never take a bus or a taxi, with everything they want to see within walking distance of most hotels. Staying around Toompea, the hill on which old Tallinn is built, can occupy a leisurely three–four-days' stay. Those with more time or who are staying in the suburbs will find public transport easy to use and taxis reasonably priced. Kadriorg Palace and the Rocca al Mare Open Air Museum are both on direct bus or tram routes with a fare of 30p/50c. Cycling there is a sensible alternative option. The long-distance bus station is halfway between the airport and the Old Town and is well served by local buses and trams. Day-to-day life is now totally Western so there is no need to shop in advance before coming; a forgotten toothbrush, a favourite tipple or an easy-read paperback can be bought seven days a week and even all around the clock. Indeed, most such items will be much cheaper than if bought at home.

Museums still open and close to suit the staff rather than visitors and it is sad that even new museums such as KUMU (Estonian Art Museum, see page 129), the modern art museum which opened in February 2006, could not break this pattern. Most close at least one day a week – usually Monday or Tuesday – and some take

21

TALLINN

Patarei Prison
Linnahall
Heliport
Harbour Terminals A, B & C
Tourist information
Portus
Harbour Terminal D
Railway station
SADAMA
Architecture Museum
AHTRI
MERE PST
PIKK
OLD TOWN (VANALINN)
Coca-Cola Plaza
Forum
Central
Central post office
VIRU
Viru
Tallink
PARNU MNT
GONSIORI
ESTONIA PST
SAS Radisson
RAVALA PST
A LAUTERI
TARTU
JOE
PRONKSI
NARVA MNT
RAUA
St John's Almshouses
Olümpia
LIIVALAIA
Park
GONSIORI
J VILMSI
POSKA
Keila, Paldiski
LIIVALAIA
Keila, Paldiski
VEERENNI
Central market
JUHKENTALI
TARTU MNT
Kalevi Stadium
Bus station
Siselinnu Cemetery
Sõjaväe Cemetery
© Bradt Travel Guides Ltd

Bay of Tallinn

Maarjamäe Palace
Viimsi
PIRITA TEE
Exhibition Centre
Narva
Song Festival Amphitheatre
Russalka Memorial
NARVA MNT
SADAMA
KADRIORG
Kadriorg Park
Kadriorg Palace
Peter the Great Museum
WEIZENBERGI
Park Museum
Narva
LASNAMÄE TEE
Mikkel Museum
KUMU (Estonian Art Museum)
LAAGNA TEE
LAAGNA TEE
Kadriorg Stadium
N
Bradt
PAE
PUNANE
LASNAMÄE
PALLASTI
MAJAKA
PAE
Nar
PETERBURI TEE
Su
Ülemiste Station
SUUR - SÕJAMÄE
Airport, Tartu
Lake Ülemiste
Ülemiste

0 _____ 400m
0 _____ 400yds

two days off. They also close on public holidays. If visiting one is crucial to your holiday, check first that it is open when you plan to be there. Churches are, of course, open every day so they can always provide the backbone to a visit.

Since around 2001, Tallinn has consistently enjoyed an ever-increasing number of tourists on a year-round basis. The new hotels that open are soon filled and the arrival of no-frills airlines in 2004 expanded the market further. Perhaps 2007 will see something of a plateau as the effects of the constant and very positive publicity that promoted Tallinn around the time of EU accession in 2004 wear off. 2006 has seen about 350 new rooms in Tallinn in a wide range of hotels so prices, particularly in winter, may start to fall again. There will certainly be further new hotels in 2007.

WHEN TO VISIT

Tallinn is a very different city in the two major seasons of winter and summer. In the former, tourists enjoy themselves largely indoors around a programme of concerts, ballet and filling meals. In the summer, when daylight reduces the night to an hour or two, the attractions are all out of doors. Some visitors probably spend their whole stay on Town Hall Square now that so much entertainment is centred there, but the more sensible will climb the walls and towers, meander through the Kadriorg Palace Gardens and take bus trips along the seashore.

Summer visitors are entertained with brass bands, fancy dress and outdoor singing. Winter ones are inspired with organ recitals, opera and chamber music.

Serious Estonians take long summer holidays so do not expect much culture in Tallinn in July or August. It is the season to unwind and have fun.

SUGGESTED ITINERARIES

ONE DAY Spend the whole day in the Old Town starting at the top of the Toompea Hill around 09.00 when the churches open but before the cruise passengers are brought there. Start at the Alexander Nevsky Cathedral (see page 150 [3 B6]), continue to the Dome Church (see page 151 [3 B5]), walk down Lühike jalg ('Short Leg') and drop into the Adamson-Eric Museum (see page 124 [3 C5]) at the bottom of the hill to be amazed at how one man could produce art in so many shapes and forms. A visit to Niguliste Church (St Nicholas's) (see page 153 [3 C5]) should finish the morning.

Spend midday around Town Hall Square and, if the weather permits, climb the Town Hall Tower for a view of contemporary Tallinn before going down to the basement (see page 148 [2 C4]) to see the exhibition on how the square has looked over the last 800 years. Do not forget to use the toilets here as they offer the best views of the foundations.

Continue the afternoon at the City Museum (see page 126 [2 C3]) and allow an hour to watch all the films which relive the bombing in 1944 and the independence demonstrations in 1988–91. Have a cup of tea in the café at the top and then finish up at the Maritime Museum (see page 139 [2 C1]) to see how and why so many nations fought for control of the harbour. Only the British (and the Estonians!) are presented in a favourable light. The latest exhibit covers the tragedy of the *Estonia* which sank in September 1994, claiming 850 lives. The two streets that link the museum to the Viru Gate, Uus and Müürivahe, are ideal for a final stroll, as they have a range of buildings to admire, but also small cafés and shops. Do take a walk around the Old Town after sunset to see the major buildings bathed in floodlight.

Tallinn Old Town

TWO DAYS After a totally urban day, some greenery is called for, so start by taking the tram to Kadriorg Palace (see page 134 [1 D2]) and linger in the gardens before going in. Do not miss the porcelain at the Mikkel Museum (see page 139 [1 D3]) before walking on to KUMU (see page 129 [1 D3]), the new art museum that opened in February 2006. A rest will be needed before setting off further out of town to the Song Festival Grounds (see page 170 [1 D2]).

Try to imagine 5,000 people singing here, or come in July 2009 and see the real thing. Take the bus back to Vabaduse Väljak (Freedom Square, [3 D6]), an area where there are many cafés for lunch. Look in at the Tallinn Art Hall to see which contemporary artists are in favour, and then face the Occupation Museum (see page 142 [3 C7]) which shows the horrors and banalities of life under the Soviet and German occupations between 1940 and 1991. Finish the afternoon at the National Library (see page 140 [3 C8]). Hopefully there will be a concert in the early evening either at Niguliste (see page 153 [3 C5]) or at the Dome Church (see page 151 [3 B5]). Choose whatever cuisine you like for dinner; in Tallinn now, it is bound to be available.

TOUR OPERATORS

In the UK, an increasing number of city-break operators are adding Tallinn to their programmes. They are joining operators who have specialised in the Baltic states since their independence. Those in the latter category offer both short breaks and longer tours around the country. Operators listed outside the UK, of course, offer more extensive programmes than city breaks, given the time passengers are likely to spend in the area. Passengers arriving late in the evening at the airport should ensure that their travel agent books an arrival transfer as there may not be enough taxis for all the passengers who want them. All operators listed below have several years' experience in the area and are fully bonded to protect the money clients have paid. They will not only have reduced airfares to the area, but often also lower hotel prices than those generally available to the public.

UK CITY-BREAK OPERATORS
Cresta Tabley Court, Victoria St, Altrincham WA14 1EZ; ☎ 0870 238 7711; f 0161 385 4059; e websales@bcttravelgroup.co.uk; www.crestaholidays.co.uk
Kirker Holidays 4 Waterloo Court, 10 Theed St, London SE1 8ST; ☎ 0870 112 3333; f 0870 066 7797; e travel@kirkerholidays.com; www.kirkerholidays.com

Traveleditions 69–85 Tabernacle St, London EC2A 4BD; ☎ 020 7251 0045; f 020 7251 7399;
e tours@traveleditions.co.uk; www.traveleditions.co.uk

BALTIC SPECIALISTS
UK
Baltic Adventures 1 Hyde Close, Harpenden, Herts AL5 4NB; ☎ 01582 462283; f 01582 764339;
e info@balticadventures.co.uk; www.balticadventures.co.uk
Baltic Holidays 40 Princess St, Manchester M1 6DE; ☎ 0845 070 5711; f 0870 120 2973;
e info@balticholidays.com; www.balticholidays.com
Baltics and Beyond 73 Lower Market St, Broad Bottom, Cheshire SK14 6AA; ☎ 0845094 2125;
e info@balticsandbeyond.com
Fregata Travel 177 Shaftesbury Av, London WC2H 8JR; ☎ 020 7420 7305; f 020 7420 7306;
e fregata@commodore.co.uk; www.fregatatravel.co.uk
Operas Abroad The Tower, Mill Lane, Rainhill, Prescot, Merseyside L35 6NE; ☎/f 0151 493 0382;
e info@operasabroad.com; www.operasabroad.com
Regent Holidays 15 John St, Bristol BS1 2HR; ☎ 0870 499 0439; f 0117 925 4866; e regent@
regent-holidays.co.uk; www.regent-holidays.co.uk
Specialised Tours 4 Copthorne Bank, Copthorne, Crawley, West Sussex RH10 3QX; ☎ 01342 712785; f 01342
717042; e info@specialisedtours.com; www.specialisedtours.com
Vamos 2 Styles Cl, The Royal, Leamington Spa, Warks CV31 1LS; ☎ 0870 762 4017; f 0870 762 1016;
e info@vamostravel.com; www.vamostravel.com

US

Amest Travel 16 Ocean Parkway #19, New York 11218; ☏ +1718 972 2217; f +1718 851 4175;
e info@amest.com; www.amest.com
Value World Tours Plaza del Lago Bldg, Suite 203, 17220 Newhope St, Fountain Valley, CA 92708; ☏ +1714
556 8258; f +1714 556 6125; e travel@vwtours.com; www.vwtours.com
Vytis Tours 40–24 235th St, Douglaston, New York 11363; ☏ +1800 778 9847 or +1718 423 6161; f 718
423 3979; e tours@vytistours.com; www.vytistours.com

Canada

Valhalla Travel and Tours 245 Pefferlaw Rd, Pefferlaw, Ontario L0E 1N0; ☏ +1800 265 0459 or +1905 737
0300; f +1905 737 0304; e info@valhallatravel.com; www.valhallatravel.com

RED TAPE

By 1994, only three years after re-establishing independence, Estonia had
become a Western country. Visas for most tourists had been abolished or were
easily available on arrival, red and green exits at customs had been established
and the major Scandinavian chains were marketing their goods all around the
country. Visitors coming to Tallinn early in the 21st century will find it hard to
visualise what a backwater it had become for much of the 20th, when the Soviet
Union first banned completely and then severely restricted all contacts with
foreigners.

Visitors from all EU countries, Australia, Canada, New Zealand, Norway, Switzerland and the US do not need visas and this list increases year by year. At the time of writing in late 2006, Estonia was planning to join the Shengen Agreement, together with Latvia and Lithuania in October 2007. Up-to-date information is available on the Ministry of Foreign Affairs site (*www.vm.ee*). Travellers who do need visas must get them from an Estonian embassy abroad so should plan their travel arrangements accordingly. They must take account of both local and Estonian holidays when embassies may be closed.

E ESTONIAN EMBASSIES OVERSEAS *For embassies in Tallinn, see page 45.*

Australia 86 Louisa Rd, Birchgrove, New South Wales 2041; ☎ 2 9810 7468; f 2 9818 1779;
e eestikon@ozemail.com.au
Canada Suite 210, 260 Dalhousie St, Ottawa K1N 7E4; ☎ 613 789 4222; f 613 789 9555;
e estonianembassy@rogers.com; www.estemb.ca
Finland Itainen Puistotie 10, Helsinki 00140; ☎ 9 622 0260; f 9 622 0261; e embassy.helsinki@mfa.ee;
www.estemb.fi
France 46 Rue Pierre Charron, Paris 75008; ☎ 1 56 62 22 00; fax 1 49 52 05 65;
e embassy.paris@mfa.ee; www.est-emb.fr
Germany Hildebrandstrasse 5, 10785 Berlin; ☎ 30 254 60600; f 30 254 60601;
e embassy.berlin@mfa.ee; www.estemb.de
Ireland Riversdale Hse, Ailsbury Rd, Dublin 4; ☎ 1 219 6730; f 1 219 6731; e embassy.dublin@mfa.ee

Latvia Skolas 13, Riga 1010; ✆ 781 2026; f 781 2029; e embassy.riga@mfa.ee; www. estemb.lv
Lithuania Mickeviciaus 4a, Vilnius 2004; ✆ 278 0200; f 278 0201; e embassy.vilnius@mfa.ee; www.estemb.lt
South Africa 16 Hofmeyr St, Welgemoed 7530; ✆ 21 913 3850; f 21 933 2579
UK 16 Hyde Park Gate, London SW7 5DG; ✆ 020 7589 3428; f 020 7589 3430; e embassy.london@mfa.ee; www.estonia.gov.uk
US 2131 Massachusetts Av, Washington, DC 20008; ✆ 202 588 0101; f 202 588 0108; e emb.washington@mfa.ee; www.estemb.org

GETTING THERE AND AWAY

✈ **BY PLANE** From around 2000, **Estonian Air** (UK ✆ *020 7333 0196; www.estonian-air.ee*) embarked on a programme of massive expansion, firstly in the hands of Maersk Air and then from 2003 under the ownership of SAS. By 2006, it had direct flights to Amsterdam, Barcelona, Berlin, Copenhagen, Kiev, London, Moscow, Paris and Stockholm, usually on a daily basis. CSA Czech Airlines, Finnair, Lufthansa and SAS also have regular services. EasyJet started a daily service to Tallinn from London in autumn 2004. Travel agents specialising in the area can also arrange for flights to Tallinn, combined with a one-way fare from another town in the Baltics. Travellers from the British Isles who do not live in London can take advantage of Lufthansa and SAS flights from Birmingham, Dublin, Edinburgh, Glasgow and Manchester to Copenhagen, Frankfurt or Stockholm and then change to Tallinn services there. CSA also operate from Stansted, Birmingham, Manchester and Edinburgh; with a careful choice of flights it is possible to have the best part of a day in Prague en route to Tallinn. Finnair have flights to Helsinki from London, Manchester and Edinburgh with onward connections to Tallinn.

Fares fluctuate frequently and for short-break visitors it is often cheaper to book a package than flights and hotels separately. The lowest fares are usually available in winter, spring and autumn, but invariably increase over Christmas and Easter. To secure reasonable prices in the summer, it is important to book well in advance. When in Tallinn, Estonian Air have a dedicated phone number for English speakers (↘ 640 1163), which is available 09.00–20.00 seven days a week.

For travellers from the US, SAS and Finnair offer good connections, again via Copenhagen, Stockholm and Helsinki, but given the very low fares usually available to London from Canada and the US, it may often be cheaper to break a journey in London and take a separate package from there. Via London is always the best route for tourists from Australia and New Zealand. With Estonian Air in Tallinn, it is possible to check in at any time of day, and also the previous day up to 21.00. This is a useful facility for clients booked on early-morning departures or those with a tight schedule before a later flight.

BY HELICOPTER FROM HELSINKI An hourly service to Helsinki operates Monday–Friday between 07.30 and 20.00 from the heliport on the roof of the Linnahall Concert Hall, next to the seaport. Flying time is 18 minutes. A reduced service operates at weekends. Various fares are offered and journeys starting in Tallinn are usually cheaper than those starting in Helsinki. For a round-trip journey, expect to pay £120–180/US$180–270. Discounts are also offered for reservations made in advance. This can be done through most travel agents or directly with the company operating the service, **Copterline**, whose office is at the heliport (↘ 610 1818; f 641 2276; e copterline@copterline.ee; www.copterline.ee). For personal bookings they also have an office in the Viru Hotel.

BY FERRY FROM HELSINKI

Competition between an increasing number of companies on the Tallinn–Helsinki route ensures a year-round comprehensive service, supplemented in the summer by catamarans which reduce the journey time to 90 minutes. Most ferries take about three to four hours and in good weather the views of Helsinki and Tallinn make this journey really worthwhile. As fares change frequently, tickets are best bought from agents in either Helsinki or Tallinn who will know the full range available. Expect to pay around £20–30/US$30–45 for a round-trip ticket. The Tallinn port site (www.portoftallinn.com) is the best starting point for an indication of services and fares. **Eckerö**, **Silja Line** and **Tallink** are the main ferry companies whilst **Linda Line** and **Nordic Jet** run the catamarans. Tallink bought Silja Line in the summer of 2006 so the Silja name will gradually be withdrawn.

Given the speed of the catamarans, a day trip in summer to Helsinki is a very practical add-on to a visit to Tallinn. (See page 187 for a suggested walk in Helsinki.) Money can be exchanged on board but exchange rates are poor so it is better to use banks or bureaux de change in either town centre. Tallinn port is within walking distance of the town and metered taxis are always available. Local buses are few and far between at the port itself in Helsinki but several routes operate within 400m or so of the port entrance.

BY BUS The bus station (**Autobussijaam**) for domestic and international departures is on Lastekodu, off the Tartu road which leads to the airport. Plans were announced in 2006 that it would in due course move to what is now the car park for the Ülemiste shopping centre, but this is unlikely to happen during the currency of this edition. The phone number for enquiries is 680 0900 but do not expect English to be spoken.

Eurolines are the main operator of international services although they are now beginning to face competition. They operate five times a day to both Riga and St Petersburg and keep to their timetables as they always have priority at the border. Some of the buses to Riga continue to Vilnius and Minsk. Their timetables are available online at www.eurolines.ee and they are also published in *Tallinn In Your Pocket*. Tickets can be booked online, through travel agents before arrival or at their office at the bus station in Tallinn. Tickets booked at the bus station will cost about £15/US$28 to St Petersburg and £10/US$18 to Riga but agents will of course add a service charge to this.

There is an extensive domestic bus service from Tallinn to towns all over Estonia. Fares right across the country will not exceed £7/US$12 and full timetables and fares are displayed at the bus station. It is not normally necessary to book in advance but this should be done for services on Friday and Sunday evenings and also on major holidays. Only one-way tickets are sold so the return ticket to Tallinn should be bought on arrival at the destination. On the main routes there is competition and savings can be made by adjusting travel timings to the buses of the cheaper operators. In the summer of 2006, tickets for a limited number of routes started to be sold online.

BY TRAIN Train services declined consistently after independence for many years but improvements started in 2005, in particular on the service to Tartu. More trains are likely to Narva, although the through service to St Petersburg finally stopped in 2005. In 2006, there was still a daily overnight service to Moscow.

✚ HEALTH

No inoculations are required and hygiene standards in hotels and restaurants are high. Nevertheless, it would be sensible here, as at home, to be up to date with immunisations against diphtheria and polio. It is wise to carry a good insect repellent and to use it day and night if mosquitoes are around. Local hospitals can be trusted to deal with any emergency; long gone are the days when foreigners flew to Helsinki or Stockholm for any minor ailment. EU passport holders are entitled to use health facilities in the Baltic states on the same basis as residents.

TRAVEL CLINICS AND HEALTH INFORMATION A full list of current travel clinic websites worldwide is available on www.istm.org. For other journey preparation information, consult www.tripprep.com. Information about various medications may be found on www.emedicine.com/wild/topiclist.htm.

SAFETY

Violent crime is very rare in Tallinn although drunken brawls late on Friday and Saturday nights can be unpleasant. It is, however, easy to avoid the rowdy clubs which generate these. Pickpockets are a problem in markets during the summer when the hordes of cruise passengers provide plenty of temptation. The 'sink' estates where, perhaps inevitably, the drug culture thrives are fortunately well away from the areas visited by tourists. Women will not feel uncomfortable walking on their own.

WHAT TO TAKE

Tallinn became very Western very quickly after independence; by around 1996, there was nothing that could not be easily bought in either a specialist or a department store. Tourists can travel light in the knowledge that they can buy anything they need in Tallinn, often at lower cost than at home.

NOTES FOR DISABLED TRAVELLERS

Gordon Rattray; www. able-travel.com

Cobbled streets, narrow doorways and high steps make Tallinn's Old Town a challenge for travellers with mobility problems, but with some research and effort, a visit to this city is quite feasible.

ARRIVALS Assistance with an aisle chair will be provided at Tallinn Airport and there is a disabled toilet in the building. Tallinn port is also fairly accessible, with lifts, sliding doors, disabled toilets and disabled parking.

GETTING AROUND

By train Although some railway stations have ramps and access, this is not a general rule. Trains do not have disabled toilets and some platforms are so low that wheelchair travellers will need to be lifted on and off.

By bus Several new buses, trams and trolleybuses with low floors have recently been introduced, and their routes are marked in yellow on English-language timetables (see *http://soidduplaan.tallinn.ee*)

By taxi These two taxi companies have wheelchair-accessible vehicles:

Toiran \f +372 673 1933; mob: +372 522 7477; e toiran@hot.ee. The despatchers don't speak good English, so it may be better to send an email.

Tulika Takso \ +372 612 0040; f +372 612 0002; e info@tulika.ee. This service must be ordered at least one day in advance.

ACCOMMODATION All the large hotels, such as the SAS Radisson (see page 61) , the Meriton Grand (see page 60), the Olümpia (see page 61), the Viru (see page 65) and the Tallink (see page 64), have some degree of access for disabled travellers, with appropriately designed rooms. For further details, see pages 56–73. All new hotels opening in 2007 will be similarly equipped.

FURTHER INFORMATION An excellent online resource, providing detailed information (including photos) on all aspects of accessibility in Tallinn is http://liikumisvabadus.invainfo.ee. This site is available in English and is being constantly updated.

Tallinn City Board of Disabled People (\ +372 655 4160; e koda@tallinnakoda.ee) provides advice for disabled people.

Tallinn Tourist Information Centre (\ +372 645 7777; f +372 645 7778; e turismiinfo@tallinnlv.ee; www.tourism.tallinn.ee) can give general information.

$ MONEY AND BUDGETING

CURRENCY The Estonian kroon is tied to the euro at the rate of 15.65EEK. In December 2006, exchange rates against the pound and US dollar were £1 = 23.40EEK and US$1 = 12.27EEK. Notes are issued for 2, 5, 10, 25, 50,100 and 500EEK. There are also coins for 10, 20, 50 sents and for one kroon.

BUDGETING Hotel costs in Tallinn will be similar to those in western Europe or the US, outside the big cities. Do, however, remember that room rates always include a substantial buffet breakfast. All other expenditure, mainly meals and transport, will be much cheaper. Allow around 50p/80c for coffee and a similar amount for cakes. Estonians have not yet adopted take-away food on a large scale; they either prepare it in their offices and homes or eat out. Restaurants do not offer set-price meals so eating is always à la carte, although a number now have a dish of the day, 'päeva praad', which is usually cheaper than anything else. Great savings can be made by avoiding wine with meals and drinking beer instead. Most restaurants charge the same at lunch as in the evening although a few glamorous restaurants have a 'business lunch' to encourage midday trade. In most restaurants in central Tallinn allow about £2/US$3 for a starter, £5/US$8 for the main dish and £3/US$5 for the sweet. Much lower prices can be found away from the Old Town and the port where prices are governed by the number of tourists and expats in the area.

Many tourists use a taxi or public transport only to get to and from the airport.

Most hotels are within walking distance of many of the sights tourists will want to visit. As a carnet of ten bus tickets costs 85EEK (£3.50/US$6), little needs to be allowed for travel for those who venture further.

TIPPING It is normal to leave 10% in restaurants, cafés, taxis and hairdressers when the service is good. Many expats make a point of not tipping if the service does not deserve it, in the hope that it will improve on future occasions!

Bradt Travel Guides is a partner to the 'know before you go' campaign, masterminded by the UK Foreign and Commonwealth Office to promote the importance of finding out about a destination before you travel. By combining the up-to-date advice of the FCO with the in-depth knowledge of Bradt authors, you'll ensure that your trip will be as trouble-free as possible.

www.fco.gov.uk/travel

3 Practicalities

$ BANKS AND CREDIT CARDS

The **Hansapank** at Suur-Karja 1/Vana Turg 2 and the **Äripank** at Vana Viru 7, close to the Viru Gate [2 E3], usually give the best exchange rate for pounds and dollars. The nearby **Tavid** Exchange at Aia 5 [2 E3] is very useful for getting rid of unwanted notes from all over the world. During the day, their rates are as good as those at Äripank and they do not charge commission so even small amounts can sensibly be exchanged. Tavid is open around the clock but from 19.00 until 09.00 the following day during the week, and from 17.00 at the weekends, their rates worsen considerably, often by as much as 10%. In November 2005 they opened an office at Dunkri 1, just beside Town Hall Square. Rates here are good provided a minimum sum is exchanged, usually around £60/US$100. Elsewhere in the town, both at banks and exchange bureaux, the rate for pounds can vary enormously whereas that for dollars and euro is less erratic. There are many exchange bureaux and banks along Viru [2 D4] which leads from Viru Square to Town Hall Square. Check the rates before deciding which to use. The exchange bureaux are open daily from 10.00 until 19.00. Banks close at 17.00 or 18.00 and do not usually open at weekends, except for those branches based in large shopping centres which open on both Saturday and Sunday. ATMs (cashpoints) are available throughout the town.

Appalling rates for all currencies can always be guaranteed at the 'airside' bureau in Tallinn Airport and at the bus station so these two outlets should be avoided. The banks 'landside' at the airport and those at the railway station usually offer reasonable rates. Tourists are advised not to accept notes of 500EEK when changing money since they are often difficult to use as most transactions will involve much smaller sums or can be paid by credit card.

Tourists from Britain can obtain kroon at Gatwick Airport before they leave and from all major banks. They are also available in Helsinki. This also applies for the two other Baltic currencies. Very few shops in Tallinn accept foreign currency, as it is technically illegal for them to do so. Exchange bureaux never accept travellers' cheques and few banks do either. They are equally useless in shops and hotels. Leave them at home!

CREDIT CARDS As credit cards are now widely used, there is no need to change large sums of money. Cards may be used in all hotels and restaurants, and in most shops. Few museums and galleries are able to accept them, although those that have opened recently usually do. Bus and train tickets, even those on international routes, have to be paid for in cash, but the cost of these is very low.

LOCAL MEDIA

The *Baltic Times*, published weekly on a Thursday, is the best English-language source of news for the three Baltic republics. It also lists exhibitions and concerts. *Tallinn In Your Pocket*, published every two months, is invaluable for its independent – and therefore irreverent – reviews of restaurants, museums and other sites. The *City Paper*, also published every two months, covers Tallinn, Riga and Vilnius together in a similar way to *Tallinn In Your Pocket* but with the addition of political articles. The printed version now concentrates more on background articles, but their website has a full and critical list of hotels and restaurants. Both the *City Paper* and *Tallinn In Your Pocket* are a welcome contrast to many worthy but dull local guidebooks. Travel agents abroad who specialise in the Baltics will be able to provide copies of both publications or they are available online at www.inyourpocket.com and www.balticsworldwide.com. Several free-of-charge listings magazines are circulated by hotels and local travel agents but as these are supported totally by advertising, they cannot be entirely trusted. European editions of British and American newspapers are on sale in Tallinn at the larger hotels on the day of publication.

There are no local radio or television stations that transmit in English.

C COMMUNICATIONS

TELEPHONES Public phone boxes take only phonecards, which can be bought at kiosks. They do not take cash or credit cards. Calls can also be made from post offices. Mark-ups on phone calls from hotel rooms vary enormously. Some hotels have wisely reduced prices to persuade visitors not to use their mobile phones; others have kept charges that were acceptable in the 1990s but are not any longer. As in Britain, there is now no distinction in Estonia between costs for local or national calls, although some hotels still maintain one. From a phone box, reckon to spend about 40p/70c a minute to phone a landline in Britain or North America.

Dialling To reach Tallinn by phone from abroad, dial the Estonia country code 372, and then the Tallinn seven-digit number. This will always begin with a '6'. A similar system operates in other areas of Estonia. For instance, all Tartu numbers begin with a '7'. To reach phones abroad from Tallinn dial 00 and then the relevant country code.

Mobile phones Many Estonians now have mobile phones, which are operated by a number of different companies. They each have a separate access code which is dialled after the 372 and which replaces the city code of 6. Despite the popularity of mobile phones, calls to and from them are still much more expensive than those to and from landlines.

The SMS craze hit Tallinn earlier and more vigorously than most other cities. Such was the variety of services already then available that in autumn 2003 *Tallinn In Your Pocket* devoted a special section to this topic. Paying for car parks and checking bank balances this way is now old hat for Tallinners, as is checking the weather and finding a recipe for dinner. Recent additions include donating food for a baby elephant at Tallinn Zoo and buying condoms from machines that used to accept cash.

Useful telephone numbers

Ambulance and Fire Brigade	☎ 112
Central Hospital	☎ 620 7015
City Tourist Office	☎ 645 7777
Police	☎ 110
Telephone Information	☎ 626 1111

POST The **Central Post Office** is at Narva mnt 1 [1 A2], opposite the Viru Hotel. It has relatively short opening hours (*Mon–Fri 08.00–20.00, Sat 08.00–18.00; closed on Sun*). It sells postcards, changes money and provides telephone services. Tourists often use the post office at the top of the Old Town at Lossi plats 4 [3 B6] beside the Alexander Nevsky Cathedral but this too has limited opening hours (*Mon–Fri 09.00–17.00*). For collectors, it has a wide selection of stamps and postcards which are sold at much lower prices than those charged elsewhere in the Old Town. The postal service is extremely efficient, with cards reaching anywhere in Europe within a few days.

INTERNET All major hotels have a business centre offering a full range of services including internet access but the charges are high – usually around 100EEK

(£4/US$6) per half-hour. Terminals are free of charge, but therefore often in use, at the National Library [3 C8]. Kaubamaja, the department store at the back of the Viru Hotel [1 A3], charges 40EEK (£1.75/US$3) an hour; the store is open seven days a week (*Mon–Fri 09.00–21.00, Sat 09.00–20.00 and Sun 10.00–18.00*). However the café in the bus station below the Viru Centre charges 45EEK for two hours or has a ten-hour ticket which costs 100EEK. This can be used on as many visits as required until the total time is used up. Its opening hours are the same as above. By far the cheapest centre in Tallinn is **Matrix** at Tartu 31 [1 B3], on the road to the bus station and airport. It charges only 15EEK (70p/US$1) an hour and is open day and night. The clientele is largely teenagers playing computer games and looking at sites which their parents would probably try to ban at home.

The computers which used to be available for free public use at the airport have been withdrawn. Only those passengers with access to the business lounges now have this facility.

E EMBASSIES

Canada Toom-Kooli 13; ☎ 627 3311; f 627 3312; e tallinn@canada.ee [3 B6]
Ireland Vene 2; ☎ 681 1888; f 681 1899; e embassytallinn@eircom.net [2 C4]
Latvia Tõnismägi 10; ☎ 646 1313; f 631 1366 [3 D8]
Lithuania Uus 15; ☎ 631 4030; f 641 2013; e amber@anet.ee; www.hot.ee/lietambasada [2 D5]

Russia Pikk 19; ☏ 646 4175; f 646 4178; e vensaat@online.ee; www.estonia.mid.ru [2 C3]
UK Wismari 6; ☏ 667 4700; f 667 4723; e information@britishembassy.ee; www.britishembassy.ee [3 A8]
US Kentmanni 20; ☏ 668 8100; f 668 8134; e tallinn@usemb.ee; www.usemb.ee [1 A3]

Out of office hours, these phone numbers will have a recorded announcement on how to reach a member of staff in an emergency.

✚ HOSPITALS AND PHARMACIES

The Central Hospital (☏ 620 7015) on Ravi [1 A4] provides 24-hour emergency care and the 24-hour pharmacy (☏ 644 2282) is at Tõnismägi 5 [3 D8]. Long gone are the days when foreigners who fell ill demanded to be taken immediately to Helsinki.

RELIGIOUS SERVICES

Tallinn now has an active religious life, with services held regularly at all the re-functioning churches in the Old Town. An English-language service is held every Sunday at 15.00 at the Holy Ghost Church [2 C4]. Full details are available on www.eelk.ee/tallinna.puhavaimu. The synagogue is on Karu near the harbour. There is currently no mosque in Tallinn.

i TOURIST INFORMATION

The **Tallinn Tourist Board** has a shopfront office on the corner of Kullassepa and Niguliste (St Nicholas's) [2 C4] which sells a small range of books, maps and cards. They have up-to-date editions of *Tallinn In Your Pocket* and the *City Paper*. There is also a large reference folder with timetables for ferries to Finland, buses out of Tallinn and local railways. There is a similar office in the ticket hall by the harbour [1 B2]. This office, like all other tourist offices around Estonia, has a website (*www.visitestonia.com*). Visiting these sites before departure will save a lot of time on arrival.

For tourists who arrive without having pre-booked any excursions, or who need to book further accommodation in the Baltic area, the tourist office mentioned above can advise on local operators with regular programmes. Recommended ones include:

Baltic Tours Pikk 31; ☎ 630 0460; f 630 0411; e baltic.tours@baltictours.ee; www.bt.ee [2 C3]
Estonian Holidays Rüütli 28/30; ☎ 627 0500; f 627 0501; e holidays@holidays.ee; www.holidays.ee [3 C6]
Estravel Suur-Karja 15; ☎ 626 6233; f 626 6232; e incoming.team@estravel.ee; www.estravel.ee [3 D5]

THE TALLINN CARD Vigorously promoted by the tourist board and in many hotels, the Tallinn Card will suit visitors keen to visit many museums and to travel to the outlying attractions. The cost includes a free sightseeing tour, free use of public transport and free admission to all museums. For those still active in the evenings it also includes free admission to the Hollywood nightclub. However, for those taking a more leisurely approach to their stay and who are based in the town centre, it may well be cheaper to pay as you go. No reductions in the cost are made on Mondays or Tuesdays when many museums are closed, nor in the winter when some outdoor ones are less appealing. Full details of what is included can be seen on www.tallinn.ee/tallinncard. From April 2006 the cost is 130EEK for 6 hours, 350EEK for 24 hours, 400EEK for 48 hours and 450EEK for 72 hours. The card is therefore of obvious value for visitors staying three to four days in Tallinn since if they take in the more expensive museums and make some use of public transport they are likely to save much more than the cost of the pass.

4 Local Transport

TALLINN AIRPORT

The airport is only 3–4km from the town centre. The current building dates originally from 1980 as Tallinn suddenly needed to show an international face for the Olympics (sailing events were held in the Baltic) and has been modernised on several occasions to meet the demands of Western travellers since independence. An extension was under way in 2006 to cope with the enormous increase in new services that began in 2005. A local bus service operates to the town centre every quarter of an hour with the final stop behind the Viru Hotel. Several other hotels such as the Radisson and the Central are within walking distance of this stop. Tickets bought from the driver cost 15EEK (70p/US$1.10) and only local currency can be used. Tickets bought from kiosks cost 10EEK individually or 85EEK if bought in a block of ten and they are sold at the airport kiosk. On the return journey, this shop is also useful for buying sandwiches and drinks at prices much lower than those charged on the aircraft. During the day taxis are easily available. They are all metered and cost about 100EEK (£4.50/US$7) into town. Passengers arriving on late-evening flights should pre-book a transfer through their travel agent as few taxis operate then and the bus service usually finishes around 23.30. The local bus from the airport passes the main bus station (Autobussijaam), which is useful for those wanting to continue journeys beyond Tallinn. Local buses, transfer coaches and taxis must be paid for in local currency.

There is an exchange bureau airside and also one landside in the arrivals area. The airside one offered outrageous rates throughout 2005 and 2006, about 17.50EEK to the pound, when 23EEK was easily available in the town centre. There are two banks landside and the one nearer to the departures area usually offers better rates. For travellers arriving from Britain on an Estonian Air flight from Gatwick, the Thomas Cook exchange bureau at Gatwick handles Estonian kroon. There is a cashpoint in the arrivals area. There is no tourist information office or hotel-booking agency at the airport. American and British tourists plagued by high airport taxes at home will be relieved to hear that at Tallinn Airport they are minimal. Flight schedules are available on their website (*www.tallinn-airport.ee*).

TAXIS

Taxis are all metered and have a minimum fare of 35EEK. Journeys within the town centre should not cost more than 50EEK. As taxis are reasonably priced and always metered, they can be considered for long journeys. For instance, one to Lahemaa National Park, about 100km from Tallinn, is unlikely to cost more than 900EEK (£40/US$70).

Taxi companies called by phone are always cheaper than those that ply for hire on the street or park at ranks. Their cars are a little older but perfectly safe and all have meters. Taxi Raadio (☏ *601 5111*) is reliable and a journey to the airport with them rarely costs more than 60EEK. There are constant problems with taxis overcharging for the short journey from the port to hotels in the Old Town. Reasonably fit visitors may want to consider walking if they are booked at a nearby hotel, or taking the number 2 or 20 bus to Viru Square, which is very close to a large number of hotels.

LOCAL BUSES/TRAMS AND TROLLEYBUSES

Many tourists to Tallinn never take either a bus or a taxi during their stay as the Old Town is very close to most of the hotels and the steep narrow roads conveniently restrict traffic to pedestrians only anyway. Such visitors, however, miss everything that is cheaply and easily accessible by bus outside the Old Town. There are competing bus companies so exact routes and numbers change from time to time but services are frequent and the public transport map *Tallinna Ühistranspordi kaart*, published by Regio, is reprinted sufficiently often to be up to date. Some stops have maps but not all do and the names of the stops listed in the timetables are unlikely to mean much to visitors. The tram and trolleybus routes are of course fixed.

In autumn 2006 the flat fare was 10EEK for individual tickets bought from kiosks or 15EEK for tickets bought on the bus. A book of ten tickets bought at kiosks costs 85EEK, so buying one of these halves the cost of travel. Passes are available for a wide range of durations and again these are sold only in kiosks, not on the buses themselves. In 2006, these were available for one hour at 15EEK, two hours at 20EEK, 24 hours at 45EEK and 72 hours at 85EEK. With judicious planning, these can provide a wide range of travel, including reaching the port, bus station or airport on departure. (See also *The Tallinn Card*, page 46.) Good bus services operate to Pirita and Rocca al Mare and also to the cheaper suburban hotels such as the Dzingel and Susi. Tram enthusiasts will be pleased at the number of places relevant to tourists which their routes pass.

CAR HIRE

This is not advisable within Tallinn. Distances are so short and parking so difficult that public transport, taxis and bicycles are the sensible way to get around. Visitors planning to travel to other towns can easily rely on buses but cars are very useful for seeing the coast and national parks. In the summer it is important to pre-book cars as demand invariably exceeds supply. Tour operators abroad can easily do this, as can the local agents listed above, or bookings can be made directly with the many international and local companies now involved in this business.

CYCLING

This is a very sensible way of visiting the city, particularly as many places in the Old Town are difficult to reach by car and buses of course cannot travel on the narrow roads there. Much of the town is very flat and the rides out to Pirita or Rocca al Mare offer scenic and architectural perspectives not available in the centre. **City Bike** (↘ *683 6383 or 511 1819;* e *mail@citybike.ee; www.citybike.ee*) have daily group tours around Tallinn and also arrange transport for cyclists to Lahemaa National Park or Paldiski. In May 2006, they opened an office and a hostel at Uus 33 in the Old Town where tours start and where the bicycles are stored.

As cycling is impractical around the top of the Old Town, the company organises 'Nordic walks' (walking with a pole) which aims to combine exercise with pleasure.

5 Accommodation

Tallinn now has about 60 hotels but they are often fully booked at weekends, during trade fairs and in the peak summer season. Pre-booking is therefore always advisable. Specialist travel agents abroad often have access to lower prices than those quoted by the hotels directly, and they may also have allocations at several hotels specifically reserved for them. February 2001 saw the opening of the Radisson and during 2002 and 2003 several smaller hotels opened in the Old Town and just outside it, whilst 2004 saw the opening of the 200-room Tallink Hotel opposite the Viru Hotel, L'Ermitage next to the National Library and the Ülemiste beside the airport. There was little new in 2005 with only one major development, the Merchant's House which may well have many successors in future years as hotels convert Old Town properties into quiet oases from the bustle outside. The years 2006 and 2007 will see several hotels taking advantage of the laxer planning environment recently introduced in Tallinn. The council is happy to see more skyscrapers and less control over renovation in the Old Town.

The recommendations that follow are obviously rather arbitrary and omission of a hotel should in general be taken as resulting from lack of space rather than necessarily as a criticism. An ethical tour operator will be able to warn visitors away from the fortunately few hotels that have degenerated into brothels, which sadly cannot be listed as such here, much as though one is tempted to take the risk. It can be assumed in all cases that the rooms in the hotels mentioned below have private facilities, that the hotel accepts credit cards, and that it has a restaurant and bar. Many hotels have saunas which guests can use free of charge. Baths are rare in Estonian hotels, even in four-star establishments, so should be specifically requested. By the time this book is published, probably all the hotels will be giving free Wi-Fi (wireless internet) access to their guests.

PRICES

In luxury hotels expect to pay around £125/US$190 a night, in first class £70/US$120 and in tourist class £35–60/US$60–100. The more expensive hotels sometimes reduce prices at weekends and in July, the local holiday season, whereas the cheaper hotels usually increase them then. Prices always include a buffet breakfast. Until 2005 hotels made little effort to fill their rooms in the low season. Winter 2005–06 saw a drastic change in this policy, with discounts of 50% on the summer rates very common. November, late January and February are the months when the best rates are offered.

The prices quoted in EEK in this section should be taken as a rough indication of the price for a standard twin/double room with breakfast. Like airline fares, these vary enormously according to which agency makes the booking, the time of year, the day of the week and how far in advance the booking is made. The Estonian kroon is tied to the euro at a rate of €1 = 15.65EEK. In December 2006, £1 = 23.40EEK and US$1 = 12.27EEK.

Rock-bottom accommodation is hard to find in Tallinn, as is bed and breakfast. There is neither the wherewithal nor the will to make Tallinn backpacker friendly. Most Estonian families do not have a dining room, let alone a spare bedroom, so cannot rent out rooms. Rundown buildings which elsewhere might be converted to hostels are in Tallinn quickly transformed into offices or exclusive private houses. The increasing number of small hotels that are opening is again unlikely to stimulate demand for inferior accommodation at a not much lower price. The *Tallinn In Your Pocket* website (*www.inyourpocket.com*) always has an up-to-date list of hostels and agencies for arranging long stays in private houses.

Street scene

The word 'hotell' in Estonian has a double 'l' in the spelling. Some use this in their email and web addresses, whilst others adopt the English spelling with one 'l'.

LUXURY

🏠 **Schlössle** (27 rooms) Pühavaimu 13/15; ☎ 699 7700; f 699 7777; e schossle@consul-hotels.com; www.consul-hotels.com [2 C3]

Formerly known as the Parkconsul Schlösse, this hotel was for several years in a class on its own. Competition finally came in 2003 with the opening of the Three Sisters (see below) and more will come with the opening of the Telegraaf in December 2006. A townhouse owned by many successful Baltic Germans over the years, the Schlössle was converted into Tallinn's first truly luxurious hotel and any senior government minister from abroad has always stayed here. It is small enough to maintain the air of a gracious private residence. There is a small conference centre, but it seems incongruous. The hotel is a setting for constant but unostentatious indulgence, for cigars rather than cigarettes, for champagne rather than wine. The restaurant, like all the best ones in Tallinn, is in a cellar and has an extensive menu. For those able briefly to abandon all this indulgence, the hotel is within walking distance of all the attractions in the Old Town. *Dbl 3,350EEK.*

🏠 **Telegraaf** (80 rooms) Vene 9; 📞 600 0600; f 600 0601; e info@telegraafhotel.com; www.telegraafhotel.com [2 C3]
When this opens in December 2006, it will be Tallinn's largest 5-star hotel. Unusually for the Old Town, it will offer a small swimming pool, spa rooms and underground car-parking facilities. Strict planning controls have ensured that the 19th-century façade from what was the main post office has been maintained. *Dbl 3,000EEK.*

🏠 **Three Sisters** (23 rooms) Pikk 71; 📞 630 6300; f 630 6301; e info@threesistershotel.com; www.threesistershotel.com [2 C1]
Perhaps because it is so luxurious, the hotel does not bother with an Estonian name as no Estonian could afford it. It is clearly aiming to rival the Schlössle and is to some extent modelled on it. Both buildings have a history of over 500 years and both can claim famous rather than notorious owners. Here a library is the dominating public room and a member of staff escorts guests into the lift for the one-floor journey down to the restaurant. With only a small number of rooms, one even with a piano, the atmosphere of a 19th-century

townhouse can still be maintained. Computers and plenty of other 21st-century paraphernalia are available if needed, but it seems a pity to let modernity intrude. Estonians who wish to impress their friends on the cheap come for lunch here and linger over a £5/US$8 club sandwich. Foreigners come in the evening for pumpkin soup, pork with chanterelle mushrooms and a particular rarity in Estonia, homemade ice cream. Queen Elizabeth II stayed here in October 2006. *Dbl 5,550EEK.*

🏠 **Viru Inn** (15 rooms) Viru 8; ☎ 644 9167; f 641 8357; e viruinn@viruinn.ee; www.viruinn.ee [2 D4]
It is perhaps surprising that this is the first hotel to convert an old townhouse as carefully as possible into a boutique hotel. It opened in May 2006 with beams providing constant obstruction, such is the eagerness to preserve rather than to convert. Access is difficult for both the old and the very young, given the number of stairs and the length of the corridors. Needless to say, there is of course no lift. The positive side of this is that the fit and middle aged will enjoy an escape from all-too-modern Viru St back into the 19th century and the assurance that no families or rowdy youngsters will disturb them there. Good soundproofing ensures their isolation. The Al Sole café downstairs provides a halfway house between the old and the new, with light meals and cakes worthy of its more famous competitors. Its décor and quiet music should deter stag groups. *Dbl 2,500EEK.*

FIRST CLASS

🏠 **Barons** (34 rooms) Suur-Karja 7; ☎ 699 9700; f 699 9710; e barons@baronshotel.ee; www.baronshotel.ee [3 D5]
For every bank that closes in Tallinn, a new hotel opens, but in this case it is on the same site. Thirteen different banks in fact occupied the building during the 20th century. Some doors as a result do seem

excessively secure. Visitors will find it hard to believe that the Barons opened in 2003 rather than 1903, since the panelling, the minute lift, the sombre colour schemes and the illustrations of Tallinn are all from the earlier date. So is the name of the road: '*karjatama*' means 'to herd', as cattle used to be led to pasture along it. Whenever renovation is carried out, more and more papers from the early 20th century come to light. The view from many rooms and from the restaurant over the Old Town will again keep the 21st century away. For once it is sensible to go upstairs to eat in Tallinn, rather than downstairs. Do however avoid Fri and Sat nights here, when the hotel is an oasis of quiet against a backdrop of raucous behaviour in the surrounding bars. No rooms have baths but the suites have jacuzzis. *Dbl 2,500EEK.*

🏠 **Domina City** (68 rooms) Vana-Posti 11–13; ✆ 681 3900; f 681 3901; e city@domina.ee; www.dominahotels.com [3 D5]

As one of the few hotels to open in 2002, the Domina, with its Old Town location, its size and its standards, was bound to succeed and none of those that have opened since can claim to compete with it. Many rooms have baths as well as showers, and for those that do not, the computers built into the TV sets will be more than adequate compensation. Some British will like the choice of Sky as well as BBC TV. Full AC will be installed during 2007–08. The Italian management is reflected in the ample use of marble in the reception area and with the range of wildly abstract art in the restaurant. What is distinctly not Italian is the fact that two whole floors are non-smoking. Like all good restaurants in Tallinn, the one here is built into a brick-lined cellar. Lovers of Soviet memorabilia should note the red star on the roof. *Dbl 2,400EEK.*

🏠 **Domina Ilmarine** (150 rooms) Pohja 23; ✆ 614 0900; f 614 0901; e ilmarine@domina.ee; www.dominahotels.ee

What was Estonia's major machine-tool factory from the Tsarist period until World War II, which then turned to making hearing aids in Soviet times, is an unlikely background for a modern, hygienic and well-lit hotel but that is the fact. So well regarded was the business during Estonia's first period of independence that both the president and the prime minister invested in it. Being just outside the Old Town, the hotel has space and uses it well. The rooms are big, as are the public areas, and there is ample parking space for coaches and for private cars. Double glazing prevents any traffic noise from causing a disturbance. Part of the hotel is allocated to flats for long-stay guests. *Dbl 2,000EEK.*

⌂ **Forum** (270 rooms) Narva mnt 1a; ☎ 605 3820; f 605 3821; e forum@nordichotels.org; www.nordichotels.org [1 A2]
Due to open in the autumn of 2007, directly opposite both the Viru and the Tallink hotels. It will compete with them for groups and business travellers. An underground car park will be a novel feature.

⌂ **Kalev Spa** (100 rooms) Aia 18; ☎ 649 3300; f 649 3301; e kalevspa@kalevspa.ee; www. kalevspa.ee [2 D2]
Around 2000, Estonians suddenly discovered they needed to keep healthy, so spas and gyms sprung up around the country, particularly on the coast. This hotel, which opened in January 2006, is the first one in a town centre so its facilities, including a very welcome swimming pool, are geared as much to residents as to visitors from outside. Their use, however, is free of charge to hotel guests. The restaurant overlooks the swimming pool which must make over-indulgent guests feel guilty. *Dbl 1,900EEK.*

⌂ **Meriton Grand** (165 rooms) Toompuiestee 27; ☎ 667 7000; f 667 7001; e hotel@grandhotel.ee; www.grandhotel.ee [2 B2]

Travellers who came to Tallinn in the early 1990s will remember the grim Hotel Tallinn that used to besmirch this site. Luckily all traces of it were removed before this new hotel opened in 1999. Being immediately below the Old Town and having more than ample rooms, it appeals both to business travellers and to tourist groups. It is tempting to spend much of a stay in this hotel in the lift, since it offers one of the best views of Toompea Hill at the top of the Old Town. British tourists are drawn by the high proportion of rooms with baths. There are plans to build a spa hotel behind the current building during 2007. *Dbl 3,000EEK.*

🏠 **Olümpia** (400 rooms) Liivalaia 33; ☎ 631 5333; f 631 5325; e olympia@revalhotels.com; www.revalhotels.com [1 A3]

Built originally for the Olympic Games in 1980, this hotel is now the firm favourite of foreign business visitors to Tallinn. With the range of restaurants and conference facilities it offers, some never leave the hotel during their stay in Tallinn. They are often joined by the local expat community which has a particular affinity for the '60s music played in the Bonnie and Clyde nightclub. At weekends and during the summer, rates drop to attract tourists paying their own way. All of the rooms are now at least of 4-star standard and the reception staff work very quickly during the arrival and departure 'rush hours'. The restaurant on the top floor offers excellent views of the Old Town and many rooms do so as well. The newspaper shop always stocks up-to-date British newspapers, a rarity in Tallinn. Tourists who want to arrive or leave in greater style than a local taxi is able to provide can hire the hotel's 9m-long Lincoln which costs about £50/US$80 an hour. *Dbl 2,300EEK.*

🏠 **SAS Radisson** (280 rooms) Rävala pst 3; ☎ 682 3000; f 682 3001; e info.tallinn@radissonsas.com; www.tallinn.radissonsas.com [1 A3]

All the main central Tallinn Hotels that opened during the 1990s were conversions of existing buildings. In 2000, the Radisson dramatically broke away from that tradition by not only starting from scratch but also by constructing what was still in early 2006 the tallest building in Tallinn. This gave it the advantage of not having to make any compromises and a purpose-built formula was worked out to appeal to both business and leisure travellers. It has often pioneered what other hotels are then forced to copy, such as free wifi for all guests. The 2005 novelty was a special low check-in for small children, with toys around should there be any delay. Cultured guests will appreciate the paintings in the lobby area by Kaido Ole, one of Estonia's best-known contemporary artists. In the same year the hotel also opened its Lounge 24, a rooftop café which gives excellent photo opportunities towards both the Old Town and the new financial area growing up (literally) in the immediate vicinity of the hotel. For tourists wanting a more unusual photo, Tallinn Central Prison is easily visible from here. The restaurants and Lounge 24 have been priced to cater for local patrons too, so are not as high as might be expected in a 4-star hotel. See page 36 for an indication of the facilities available for disabled people. *Dbl 2,500EEK.*

🏠 **Reval Park** (121 rooms) Kreutzwaldi 23; 📞 630 5305; f 630 5315; e sales @ revalhotels.com; www.revalhotels.com [1 B3]
Formerly the dreaded Kungla Hotel which could barely claim 2-star status, the site transformed itself within a few weeks during the summer of 1997 and has never looked back. It has pioneered rooms for non-smokers, for the disabled and for those with allergies as well as round-the-clock gambling, fortunately in a casino with a separate entrance. Rooms are larger here than in most other hotels and the restaurant has very low prices for excellent food. Walking to the Old Town is just about possible and indeed essential as the surroundings are very bleak. The guarded car park is free of charge to hotel guests. *Dbl 2,000EEK.*

⌂ **St Petersbourg** (27 rooms) Rataskaevu 7; ✆ 628 6500; f 628 6565; e stpetersbourg@schlosse-hotels.com; www.schlosse-hotels.com [2 B4]

The St Petersbourg is under the same management as the deluxe Schlössle Hotel and suits those who want a comfortable Old Town address and who do not miss luxury. The small number of rooms is certainly a draw. It may well be the oldest hotel in Tallinn, as it has had this role under every single regime of the 20th century. Its location near to many famous clubs and restaurants appeals to visitors who can dispense with sleep for much of the night. It is one of the very few hotels in Tallinn to offer a baby-sitting service. *Dbl 5,000EEK.*

⌂ **Santa Barbara** (53 rooms) Roosikrantsi 2a; ✆ 640 7600; f 631 3992; e st_barbara.res@scandic-hotels.ee; www.scandic-hotels.com [3 D7]

The austere limestone façade from the turn of the 20th-century hides a very professional operation which is run by the Scandic Group who also operate the nearby Palace Hotel. The cellar restaurant is completely German, with no intrusion from Estonia or anywhere else. The staff get to know all the guests, many of whom are now regulars, which makes the hotel difficult to book for first-time visitors. *Dbl 1,600EEK.*

⌂ **Savoy** (40 rooms) Suur-Karja 17-19; ✆ 680 6600; f 680 6601; e tallinnhotels@tallinnhotels.ee; www.savoyhotel.ee [3 E5]

This hotel opened in May 2006, and is under the same management as the City Portus in the harbour, but the style is completely different so it is probably just as well that the two hotels are a good mile apart. Their respective clients would mix as well as beer on wine. The Old Town location and baths in nearly all of the rooms will appeal to older tourists wanting a leisurely stay. It has many novel selling points, such as a free supply of welcome drinks in the minibar, free landline phone calls throughout Estonia, wooden shutters to keep out the summer sun, AC and handmade iron curtain-rails. The charger for laptops and mobiles has cleverly been put into the safe, so that they can be left securely in the rooms. *Dbl 2,500EEK*

🏠 **Scandic Palace** (87 rooms) Vabaduse Väljak; 📞 640 7300; 📠 640 7299; 📧 palace@scandic-hotels.com; www.scandic-hotels.com [3 E7]
The hotel brochure claims it has offered 'excellent service since 1937' and this is probably true. Although many other hotels now match its facilities, Estonians are very loyal to it as the hotel was one of the few links from the first independence period that remained throughout the Soviet era. Embassies were briefly set up in the hotel in 1991 before foreign legations could reclaim their pre-war buildings. It is now equally conveniently situated for tourists interested in the Old Town and business visitors needing the government ministries. In 1997, President Meri opened the new Presidential Suite which will doubtless for decades remain one of the most expensive in Tallinn at £250/US$400 per night, but the remaining 86 rooms are more modestly priced. The hotel is run by the Scandic Group that also operates the Santa Barbara in Tallinn, and the Ranna in Pärnu. *Dbl 2,600EEK.*

🏠 **Tallink** (300 rooms) Laikmaa 5; 📞 630 0800; 📠 630 0810; 📧 hotel@tallink.ee; www.bwhoteltallink.com [1 A3]
If this hotel had been located anywhere else in Tallinn, it would have been considered enormous, with its 300 rooms. However, as it overlooks the 500-room Viru, it seems merely large. Being closely linked to the ferry company that operates to Helsinki, it is very much an outpost of Finland in Tallinn. Everything works and the light colours are appealing, particularly in winter, but perhaps more could have been done to broaden its appeal. The bus from the airport stops outside its door and some higher rooms have good views over the Old Town. *Dbl 2,300EEK.*

⌂ **Viru** (500 rooms) Viru Väljak 4; ☎ 630 1390; f 630 1303; e viru.reservation@sok.fi; www.viru.ee [1 A3]
Being the centre of the tourism trade for much of the Soviet era, the enormous Viru initially found it hard to redefine its role in the face of competition and ever-rising standards. By 2000, it had finally undergone a complete renovation and can now serve both business clients and fastidious tourists. It has become very biased towards Finnish clients, particularly since its takeover by the Finnish chain Sokos. Some of these guests can provide unwanted liveliness late on Fri and Sat evenings. Its location is excellent for the Old Town and for local shops. Tourists determined to have a bath rather than a shower are more likely to succeed here. Although the hotel already had over 400 rooms, it opened an extension with a further 100 rooms in spring 2004. In late 2005 and through 2006 it was fighting the town council for permission to build a completely new extension to the hotel beside the neighbouring Tammsaare Park. *Dbl 2,500EEK.*

TOURIST CLASS

⌂ **Central** (247 rooms) Narva mnt 7; ☎ 633 9800; f 633 9900; e sales@revalhotels.com; www.revalhotels.com [1 A2]
This hotel became an immediate favourite of tour operators from abroad when it opened in 1995 as it had no Soviet past to eliminate. Regular improvements are consistently being made. Staff were immediately aware of the demands and eccentricities of Western tourists, who have been catered for in the café/restaurant ever since. The hotel offers disabled access and one room in the new wing is adapted for use by disabled guests. It is within easy walking distance of the Old Town and the main post office. Having opened in what was then a rundown part of town, the surrounding area is becoming increasingly attractive, with more shops and

restaurants opening every year. The restaurant Novell is in the same complex and the diversity of its food more than compensates for the drabness of its location. *Dbl 1,500EEK.*

🏠 **City Hotel Portus** (107 rooms) Uus Sadama 23; ☎ 680 6600; f 680 6601;
e tallinnhotels@tallinnhotels.ee; www.tallinnhotels.ee [1 B2]
Regular visitors to Tallinn will remember this hotel as the Saku, named after the brewery and which provided a glass of beer at check-in. If the ambience is slightly more sober now, this is undoubtedly a hotel for the young and lively. Rooms have their numbers painted on them, so that guests with uncertain late-night vision can still hopefully find the right one. It is in the port, so convenient for those also visiting Helsinki. The beer store has been converted into a children's playroom but the corridors are still painted red, orange and yellow. The Italian restaurant offers a surprisingly good meal for starting or finishing a visit to Tallinn. Bus number 20 stops outside the door, which is convenient for those who do not want to take the 15-min walk into town. *Dbl 1,000EEK.*

🏠 **Dzingel** (240 rooms) Männiku 89; ☎ 610 5201; f 610 5245; e hotell@dzingel.ee; www.dzingel.ee
Situated in Nõmme, Tallinn's most exclusive suburb, the Dzingel is in fact one of the town's simplest and largest hotels. Regular long-stay visitors find its facilities perfectly adequate in view of the low prices charged and many tourists are happy both in winter and in summer with its quiet location beside a pine forest. Modernisation in 2002 made a great difference. The bus journey north into the town centre takes about 20mins. It is one of the few hotels where the staff happily and openly speak Russian although they can manage basic English. The restaurant is dull and surprisingly expensive but there is a late-night supermarket in the same block which can provide the ingredients for a varied picnic. *Dbl 800EEK.*

L'Ermitage (91 rooms) Toompuiestee 19; ☏ 699 6400; f 699 6401; e reservations@lermitagehotel.ee; www.lermitagehotel.ee [3 A7]

Although on a main road, this hotel is in many respects quieter than others as it is so well sound proofed; late-night revellers do not get this far from the Old Town as they would actually have to walk for 10mins. It appeals to groups as coaches can stop directly in front and isn't too big as to seem impersonal. Those lucky enough to get a high room at the front will be rewarded with excellent views of the town walls. *Dbl 2,000EEK.*

Imperial (32 rooms) Nunne 14; ☏ 627 4800; f 627 4801; e imperial@baltichotelgroup.com; www.baltichotelgroup.com [2 B4]

Like the Konventa Seta in Riga, this hotel is built into the town wall, which is therefore being preserved as part of it. Although on one of the few real roads in the Old Town, the location is quiet. During 2005 the hotel was considerably upgraded which led to the demise of the stag parties who previously had been tolerated here. Rooms vary greatly in size and protruding beams sometimes add more of the medieval ambience than some guests would wish. Massive discounts are often available in winter here, together with late check-outs, useful for those booked on the afternoon flight to London. *Dbl 2,200EEK.*

Merchant's House (37 rooms) Dunkri 4–6; ☏ 697 7500; fax 697 7501; e info@merchantshousehotel.com; www.merchantshouse.com [2 C4]

In summer 2005, a formula that has worked so well in Riga at the Gutenbergs finally reached Tallinn. Woodwork dating from the 14th–16th centuries and frescoes have been integrated into a hotel that will satisfy even the most fastidious customer. Rooms of course will vary in size and shape, as do the corridors, but small detours to reach them are a small price to pay for such a special environment. Given the round-the-clock activity on Dunkri it is good that only three of the rooms face it, and that the library, which also does so, is well soundproofed. The 'winter' restaurant is amongst the cellars of the basement, the summer one in the courtyard onto which most rooms look. Tallinn's first icebar is on the ground floor and on a similar theme it is worth mentioning that all rooms have AC, an important asset for several weeks during the summer. For details of the trendy ice bar, see page 87. *Dbl 2,400EEK.*

🏠 **Meriton Old Town** (40 rooms) Lai 49; 📞 614 1300; **f** 614 1311; **e** hotel@grandhotel.ee [2 B2]
This hotel opened in March 2004 and is under the same management as the Meriton Grand, but has deliberately been pitched at a very different clientele. Those who normally shun 2- or 3-star hotels may well accept such a standard here, given the view that most rooms have either over the Old Town, of St Olav's Church, or towards the harbour. There is also the added appeal of the hotel being built into the city wall. Being on the edge of the Old Town, the place is quiet yet with a reasonably central location, within walking distance of many museums and shops. It is worth paying the slightly higher costs for the rooms on the fourth floor, with their larger size, their baths rather than showers and above all for the views. The basement rooms make up for the total lack of a view with the skilfully implanted use of the old city wall. For anyone willing to risk turning up after midnight without a reservation, rooms are then sold at half price. *Dbl 1,200EEK.*

🏠 **Mihkli** (77 rooms) Endla 23; 📞 666 4800; **f** 666 4888; **e** mihkli@anet.ee; www.mihkli.ee [3 C8]
The location on one of the main roads leading from the town centre is certainly drab and the hotel itself used to be as well. From around 1998, however, serious attempts were made to improve the décor and the

staff and these have been largely successful. It is within walking distance of the Old Town and on the doorstep of the National Library. Long-stay visitors are now here and locals use the restaurant, both of which are always a good sign. It is probably the closest hotel to the Old Town with a parking lot and the number of dedicated single rooms is helpful. The repeat business that the hotel enjoys is also evidence of a complete turnaround. The live music at the weekends in the restaurant is of a consistently high standard and is well soundproofed from the rest of the hotel. The Uniquestay group took over this hotel in Feburary 2006 so many changes can be expected. *Dbl 1,100EEK.*

⌂ **Old Town Maestro** (23 rooms) Suur-Karja 10; ✆ 626 2000; f 631 3333; e maestro@maestrohotel.ee; www.maestrohotel.ee [3 D5]
Having opened in 2001, this small hotel now has its regulars who want straightforward furnishings, peace and quiet and yet an Old Town location. Rooms are much bigger than might be expected from a converted townhouse but the lift is much smaller — it can take only one person with a case at a time. The road is traffic-free but that does mean wheeling cases along the cobbles on arrival and departure. The reception area doubles up as a bar, which adds to the family atmosphere. The sauna and the business centre are, surprisingly, side by side on the top floor. Photographers should bring their cameras for the unusual views over the town from the staircase and from the sauna. *Dbl 1,900EEK.*

⌂ **Pirita Convent Guesthouse** (21 rooms) Merivälija 18; ✆ 605 5000; f 605 5010; e pirita@osss.ee; www.piritaklooster.ee
For anyone determined to have quiet at night, this is undoubtedly the place to go for. The nuns stay up for latecomers so ideal guests are those who have dinner here and then go to their rooms. The yachting harbour

of Pirita is 3km northeast of the town and the ruined convent with this new guesthouse is set well back from the main road. Prices, too, are provincial rather than Tallinn. Tourists with a car will be happy with the space here and others will be pleased that after 500 years a religious order is finally active on the site again. An extensive programme of concerts takes place in the chapel. *Dbl 1,200EEK.*

⌂ **Shnelli** (124 rooms) Toompuiestee 37; ☎ 631 0100; f 631 0101; e reservations@gohotels.ee; www.gohotels.ee [2 A4]
As part of the much-needed renovation of the railway station, this hotel opened beside it in 2005. It is a straightforward 3-star hotel with the 'green' rooms facing the park below the Old Town and the 'blue' hopefully facing a sea and sky which display this colour, but which also overlook the platforms of the railway station. The former obviously cost rather more. The railway theme predominates in the photos on the walls and even in the design of the corridor carpets. A covered walkway links the hotel to the station and its restaurant; as with stations everywhere now, the trains are less important than the shops to which most of the space has been let. The restaurant is much cheaper than any similar one in the Old Town, and particularly at weekends offers a pleasantly quiet place to dine. There is little risk of being disturbed by the small number of trains using the station. *Single visitors hoping to change their status whilst in Tallinn may want to take advantage of the rooms only let to 2 people after midnight for 500EEK. Otherwise: green dbl 1,250EEK, blue dbl 950EEK.*

⌂ **Skane** (38 rooms) Kopli 2c; ☎ 667 8300; f 667 8301; e skane@nordichotels.ee; www.nordichotels.ee [2 A3]
Being just over the railway and the tramlines from the Old Town, this hotel is literally on the wrong side of the tracks. Hopefully gentrification of the surrounding area does not take too long and it can then look the

Old Town in the face. In the meantime guests can enjoy prices that are half of those charged by hotels just 500m away and the walk into the Old Town is very short. A tram and bus stop are on the doorstep. No rooms have baths, but all have BBC TV. *Dbl 900EEK.*

⌂ **Susi** (100 rooms) Peterburi 48; ☎ 630 3300; f 630 3400; e susi@susi.ee; www.susi.ee [1 E4]
An estate agent would probably describe the location as 'unprepossessing' since it is surrounded by factories and a petrol station and is on the wide St Petersburg motorway. It is literally the high point of Tallinn at 55m above sea level. On 14 May 1343, the St George's Night Rebellion took place here. It had started further north on 23 April and this was the nearest point to Tallinn that Estonian forces would reach. Over 10,000 were killed in a desperate attempt to overthrow the Teutonic Knights. A plaque in the hotel lobby commemorates the battle, as does the park on the other side of the road where there are several further monuments. The hotel is more comfortable and more modern than any of the other tourist-class hotels outside the centre and is easily accessible by tram. The pictures displayed on its staircase put many of Tallinn's museums to shame. There are oils, lithographs and watercolours showing contemporary and historical Tallinn; other pictures are of country scenes. They are well lit and sensibly framed and of course can be seen 24hrs a day. Should the lift break down, this gallery is more than adequate compensation. The hotel suits many groups as parking is easy, as is access to the airport and the Tartu road. *Dbl 1,000EEK.*

⌂ **Taanilinna** (20 rooms) Uus 6; ☎ 640 6700; f 646 4306; e info@taanilinna.ee; www.taanilinna.ee [2 D3]
Perhaps the owners were daring, perhaps they were foolish, but in June 2002 Tallinn saw its first hotel with Russian-speaking reception staff and with brochures in English and Russian. The spelling 'Hotell' (see page 56 for an explanation) was the only concession made to Estonia at the time, although the website now has an

Estonian section. Visitors who do not care about this will like the prices, the small number of rooms, the location in one of the few quiet streets in the Old Town and the use of wood rather than of stone. The terrace sadly looks out onto the back of a supermarket and a dreary block of flats but in future years this view may well change. The wine cellar is an unexpected bonus in a hotel of this size and category and is most welcome given the lack of other watering holes in the immediate vicinity. *Dbl 2,200EEK.*

⌂ **Ülemiste** (120 rooms) Lennujaama tee 2; ☎ 603 2600; f 603 2601; e sales@ylemistehotel.ee; www.ylemistehotel.ee [1 D4]
This hotel opened beside the airport in 2004 in what was a very bleak location but the development since then of the Ülemiste shopping centre beside it has greatly enhanced the potential pleasure of a stay here. Prices in these shops are of course much lower than those charged in the town centre. Great advantage has been taken of all the space available so expect a larger lobby, rooms and even corridors than elsewhere in Tallinn. Those able to indulge in the more expensive rooms at the top of the hotel will be rewarded with views across Ülemiste Lake. The location is very convenient given the number of flights arriving late and leaving early. It is a 400m walk to the terminal or one stop on the local bus. In the winter the hotel offers a late check-out at 15.00 to passengers taking the London flight at 16.15. For those prepared to take quite a risk, rooms are offered at half price to walk-in passengers who arrive after midnight. *Dbl 1,400EEK.*

⌂ **Unique** (67 rooms) Paldiski mnt 3; ☎ 660 0700; f 661 6176; e info@uniquestay.com; www.uniquestay.com [3 A7]
Tallinn hotels have tended to copy each other once a successful formula has been found. The larger ones inevitably copy models from abroad and the smaller ones try to recreate a 1930s ambience even though

modern technology is around if guests need it. When the Unique opened in spring 2003, it clearly wanted to break away from anything that had ever been tried before. Each room has its own flat-screen computer which can be used free of charge around the clock. It also has tea and coffee. The lighting in the corridors comes from the floor rather than the ceiling. Orange rather than green or brown is the predominant colour. Originally restricted to 17 rooms at Paldiski 3, the hotel added another 50 in April 2004 in its new building on the corner of Paldiski and Toompuiestee and plans a further extension in 2007. Several of these rooms, the Zen rooms, are as original as their predecessors, with whirlpool baths, adjustable lighting and gravity-free chairs. This is also the first hotel in Tallinn with an Estonian restaurant! The chain plans to expand both within Tallinn and to the neighbouring Baltic states and bought the Mihkli Hotel (see page 68) in February 2006. *Dbl 1,600EEK.*

🏠 **Vana Wiru** (80 rooms) Viru 11; 📞 669 1500; f 669 1501; e hotel@vanawiru.ee; www.vanawiru.ee [2 D4] Viru St is always full of tourists but most will not know of the existence of this hotel as its entrance is at the back. Potential guests should not be deterred by the fact that the building dates from the 1950s, normally the worst period of Soviet architecture. Its vast marble lobby suggests luxury but in fact most of the rooms are of a standard size and with showers rather than baths. Few have good views but with a location beside the city wall, one can forgive anything. It is certainly worth paying more for the junior suites on the fifth floor which do have extensive views over the Old Town. Shopaholics should enquire about the 10% discount the hotel arranges for its guests at the nearby Kaubamaja department store. Groups will like the convenient coach park right beside the entrance. *Dbl 1,700EEK.*

6 Eating and Drinking

There is now such a choice of restaurants in Tallinn that it is invidious to attempt a shortlist. Every major nation is represented and more unusual ones include Argentina, Georgia, Lithuania and Scotland. Hawaiian and Thai food appeared for the first time in 2000, Czech and Arabic food followed in 2002 and by 2003 Russian food had also staged a comeback, having been completely rejected in the years immediately following independence. By 2005, they were joined by an African, an Armenian and a Korean restaurant. All restaurants and bars have to provide a non-smoking section. In April 2004, there was serious discussion about following the Irish and banning smoking altogether but this had not come about by late 2006.

Detailed descriptions of restaurants appear in the *City Paper*, shorter ones in *Tallinn In Your Pocket*. A dark entrance, down poorly maintained stairs in a side street, is usually a clear indication that good food and value lies ahead. Bright lights at street level should be avoided. Exploration need no longer be limited to the Old Town; competition there is driving many new entrants to open up in the suburbs. At the time of writing, nobody has opened a revivalist Soviet restaurant, though the success of such ventures in Riga and in former East Berlin must in due course tempt some embittered members of the Russian-speaking community in Tallinn.

Most of the following restaurants have been open for several years and are popular with tourists, expats and local residents. I have, however, deliberately tried to include some that are not well known abroad and which cannot afford to advertise. I have also gambled that some new restaurants will outlive this edition of the book. Apologies in advance to the many other excellent restaurants that, with more space, would also have been included. Websites are listed so that menu planning can begin abroad and not just at the table. Restaurants are on the whole very good at keeping these up to date, and for those in a rush it is possible to pre-book not only a table but also the meal. Eating in hotels is popular in Tallinn and some of their restaurants are covered in the hotel descriptions in the previous chapter.

Restaurants usually open at 12.00 and close around midnight. Cafés open earlier, but usually only at 10.00 since Estonians do not breakfast out and as it is included in the room price in most hotels, there is no incentive for tourists to go out for it. They close around 18.00, except for those that become bars in the evening when they will stay open until midnight at least.

PRICES

Prices listed below give an indication of costs for three courses without wine (see page 38 for current conversion rate). The cost of wine varies enormously between restaurants, and is often as high as in Britain or the US. Sticking to beer saves a lot of money – and it is, after all, an Estonian national drink. A small beer is 0.3 litres and large one is 0.5 litres. On Old Town Square and in the immediate vicinity, reckon to pay about 45EEK for a small beer and 55EEK for a large one. Elsewhere 20EEK and 30EEK are the more normal charges. Excluding drink, expect to pay about 110EEK for a two-course lunch and 300EEK for a three-course dinner. Look out for the dish of the day (*paeva praad*) which normally offers particularly good value.

 **RESTAURANTS**

✕ Aed (Garden) Rataskaevu 8; ☎ 626 9088 [2 B4]
No, this is not a vegetarian restaurant but the vegetables and their sauces are what visitors remember here, particularly given that this is an all-too-common weakness in other Tallinn restaurants. Its opening during the bitter winter of early 2006 made this a particularly effective selling point. If the courtyard at the back were a little bigger, one could imagine all the herbs used growing there in pots. The large TV screens do not show football matches, nor shrieking old rock stars, but a constantly changing selection of classical paintings. It is small for the Old Town, but this is a major plus: it keeps out raucous groups. *250EEK.*

✕ African Kitchen Uus 34; ☎ 644 2555; www.africankitchen.ee [2 C1]
This restaurant became so popular during 2005 that it was hard to believe that it opened only around Christmas 2004. It is cheap and cheerful, but so much more as well. The menu is diverse, the website to the point and equality across the continent is assured by offering one cocktail, and only one, from 25 different African countries and all at the same price. Come here with a group, or be willing to become part

of one. This is not the place for dining à deux. Live music is played, with no extra costs, every Fri and Sat evening. *200EEK.*

✗ Balthasar Raekoja Plats 11; ✎ 627 6400; www.restaurant.ee [2 C4]
Garlic dominates every course here, even the ice cream, but above all in the salads. Whilst other dishes do appear on the menu, they tend to be as appetising as a vegetarian option in a steakhouse. Opening in early 2000, the restaurant took over the top floor of the former pharmacy and has kept as much of the original wooden furnishings as was practical. With the restaurant's views over the Town Hall Square, it is tempting to linger here but it also offers a quiet respite over lunch between morning and afternoon sightseeing tours. The range of short drinks at the bar can be equally tempting at other times of day. *350EEK.*

✗ Bocca Olevimägi 9; ✎ 641 2610; www.bocca.ee [2 C2]
A passer-by on the pavement here who happened to notice the plain glass windows with the two canvas panels behind them would not believe that during 2003 Bocca got more publicity abroad than all the other Tallinn restaurants put together. Only the cars parked outside suggest considerable opulence inside. Critics liked the modern minimalist layout against the medieval backdrop of very solid limestone. They liked the changing lighting schemes – and the fact that plenty of modest pasta dishes were available if octopus and veal seemed unnecessarily extravagant. The glitterati have moved on now, but standards here have stayed the same. *500EEK.*

✗ Le Bonaparte Pikk 45; ✎ 646 4444; www.bonaparte.ee [2 C2]
The formal restaurant at the back and the easy-going café at the front are both French through and through. The décor is very domestic and totally unpretentious. The care and flair all go into the food, which is still too

rare in Tallinn, whether it is a simple cake in the café or an elaborate paté at the start of a serious meal. Other unusual touches are the individual towels in the toilets and coat-warmers for visitors in winter. Prices in both the restaurant and the café are fortunately very Estonian. Those who want to take France home with them can buy a range of cheeses and bread at the counter. *450EEK.*

✗ **Cantina Carramba** Weizenbergi 20a; ☏ 601 3431; www.carramba.ee [1 C2]
Opening in Kadriorg outside the town centre in 2004 was certainly a gamble, but it has definitely paid off. The variety of Mexican food, not to mention its low cost, is certainly worth the 10-min tram ride it may take to get here. Onion rings in beer dough is one of the many original dishes served. Helpful to newcomers are the little pepper symbols beside many dishes on the menu. One indicates a medium dose where three is really strong. Being open through the day, an afternoon at the Palace or KUMU could pleasantly end with an early supper here. Do bear in mind when ordering that although the cuisine is Mexican, the portion sizes served are very American. *250EEK.*

✗ **Controvento** Katariina käik; ☏ 644 0470; www.controvento.ee [2 D3]
Uniquely in Tallinn, this restaurant could maintain a review written when it first opened in 1992. It has retained the same menu, the same décor and probably many of the same clients, who want no-nonsense home cooking in an Italian bistro and no attempts to emulate temporary culinary fads. Prices have had to increase somewhat but they remain modest in comparison with the competition in the Old Town. *300EEK.*

✗ **Eesti Maja** Lauteri 1; ☏ 645 5252; www.eestimaja.ee [1 A3]
Do not expect quick service here or even staff with much English, but instead be ready for enormous portions

and rich food at each course. It will be hard to spend more than £6/US$10 a head and many eat their fill for much less. Side rooms seating around 8–10 people are useful for private functions. One houses a collection of photographs from the 1920s. The vegetable soup makes a good meal in itself at lunchtime. The building also houses *Global Estonian*, an English-language bi-annual magazine well worth buying for the tough interviews they give to local politicians willing to meet them. *150EEK*.

✗ Golden Dragon Pikk 37; ☏ 631 3506; www.goldendragon.ee [2 C3]
This is a straightforward Chinese restaurant in the best sense of the term. The cooking is fine, the menu enormous and the service adequate, if hardly warm. Do not look forward to delicate cooking but with the prices as low as they are, it would be unreasonable to expect this. The lanterns dangle against a background of Estonian limestone. Modern China and modern Estonia share a passion for piped music so be ready for a meal to be spoiled on this account. The entrance is in a courtyard, through a heavy door and down a tortuous staircase. The complication fortunately keeps out the more raucous tourists. *180EEK*.

✗ Joujaam Väike Karja 8; ☏ 644 4984 [2 D4]
Perhaps where the Stereo Lounge started, many others will follow but in early 2006 Joujaam was the only café in the Old Town to emerge with a totally white background. The pictures and the décor all centre on the theme of electricity generation and the size of the dishes is reflected in their voltage: high for large and low for small. The smaller ones are in fact the most original; a hot salad of beans, pears and ham or a cheese-based vegetarian wrap will be remembered longer than the Adenauer pork chop or the Kekkonen steak. Hopefully these references to politicians famous in the 1950s will keep the clientele older and quieter than is normally the case in Old Town bars. *200EEK*.

✕ **Karl Friedrich** Raekoja Plats 5; ✎ 627 2413; www.restaurant.ee [2 C4]
The grand location on Town Hall Square might suggest ostentation and prices to match but fortunately this has not happened. Each floor caters for a different age group but it is the top floor that is recommended; the long walk up and down is well worthwhile. Oldies should book well in advance for a table overlooking the square and enjoy a lingering lunch or dinner. It became a pepper restaurant in 2005 so expect this ingredient even in a crème brulée or a chocolate mousse. At the same time, the kitchen moved upstairs so diners on that floor see all their food being prepared. Perhaps they went for pepper to compete with the garlic restaurant over the square? *400EEK.*

✕ **Klafira** Vene 4; ✎ 667 5144; www.klafira.ee [2 C4]
If Soviet Russia has been banished for good from Estonia, the Tsarist aristocracy is making an effective comeback here instead. Perhaps they were wise to wait until 2000, nine years after the re-establishment of Estonian independence, before doing so. Their food is strictly Russian, their wine is sensibly French. That rich Estonians are firstly willing to come and then secondly even to speak Russian to the staff shows the high standards the restaurant has set. Allow a full evening here and do not consider the cost beforehand. It will be expensive by Estonian standards, but not by London or New York ones. *400EEK.*

✕ **Kuldse Notsu Kõrts** (The Golden Pig) Dunkri 8; ✎ 628 6567; www.notsu.ee [2 C4]
Although this restaurant belongs to the St Petersbourg Hotel next door, the two establishments have nothing in common. This country restaurant, with low ceilings and long wooden tables, seems pleasantly incongruous in the middle of the Old Town. However, this is precisely its appeal. It offers varied Estonian fare – thick mushroom soups, pork in innumerable guises and apples in almost as many. Drink apple juice or beer rather

than wine. Few tourists venture in, but many Estonians do and this must be its best recommendation. *250EEK*.

✕ Liivi Steakhouse Narva mnt 1; ☎ 625 7377; www.steakhouse.ee [1 A2]

Everything is wonderfully predictable here, so this is the place to be unadventurous. All styles of steak are on the menu and they can be accompanied by a wide range of red wine. The starters are patés and soups and the sweets apple pie or ice cream. It being situated opposite the Viru Hotel in a complex that also houses the main post office means that the clientele is very varied but always conventional. *350EEK*.

✕ Lydia Koidula 13a; ☎ 629 8990; www.lydia.ee [1 C3]

Lydia pioneered the idea of genteel suburban dining in Tallinn and the proportion of locals to foreigners shows how successful they have been. However, Kadriorg is only just a suburb and a meal here makes sense after enjoying the luxury of the palace, KUMU, and the Mikkel Museum's porcelain collection. Live music means a pianist, not a band, and the décor of paintings and flowers lends itself to a leisurely, rather than a rushed, lunch or dinner. Many of the ingredients are local, but the sauces are fortunately French, so with appropriate quantities of alcohol.

✕ Meister Michel Rataskaevu 22; ☎ 641 3414; www.meistermichel.ee [2 B4]

This house belonged to Michel Sittow (1469–1525), an artist who lived for most of his life in Tallinn. He is best remembered for his portraits but sadly none of his work has remained in Tallinn itself. His portrait of Catherine of Aragon is in the Art History Museum in Vienna. Given his travels, he would have known quite a few of the varied dishes now served in this restaurant. Apples are the theme of most of them, so the results are inevitably more straightforward than in the Tallinn restaurants that take garlic or pepper as their leitmotiv instead. Children are encouraged with their special menu. *350EEK.*

✕ **Must Lammas** (The Black Sheep) Sauna 2; ☎ 644 2031; www.mustlammas.ee [2 D4]
For years this Georgian restaurant was called Exit but it changed its name in early 2001. Luckily little else has changed in the intervening years. All guests are greeted with portions of firewater and strips of salted beef as the menus are handed out. Eat meat, meat and more meat all evening, topped, if you did not have lunch, with some ice cream drenched in brandy. Start with stuffed vine leaves and move on to beef and pork stews. Vegetarians keep out. *250EEK.*

✕ **Olde Hansa** Vanaturg 1; ☎ 627 9020; www.oldehansa.com [2 C4]
Ignore the silly name and the silly costumes worn by the staff but enjoy the candles (there is no electric light) and the genuinely Estonian live music. Some tables are for two but don't venture in for a quiet, intimate evening. This is really a party venue so come as a group and with a very empty stomach. Portions are enormous, even for soup and ice cream. *300EEK.*

✕ **Peppersack** Viru tänav 2; ☎ 646 6900; www.peppersack.ee [2 C4]
Johan Peppersack was one of Tallinn's best mayors when Estonia was ruled by the Swedes in the 16th and 17th centuries. He fought the occupiers for money and for autonomy with a tenacity that no other mayor could equal in the subsequent 400 years. He would not have tolerated the mess Polish restorers, local Estonians and the Soviet occupiers got into when they tried and failed to restore the building in time for the 1980 Olympics. The compromise between Polish Baroque and the former Gothic is still there. Perhaps it

is better to look at the live entertainment, which can feature fencers, troubadours or martial artists. (Check the website if it matters which.) The menu is extensive but many find it easiest just to order one of the feasts at a fixed price which includes three courses and drink. Several of these are fish-based and one is vegetarian. *350EEK.*

✕ Sisalik (Lizard) Pikk 30; ☎ 646 6542; www.sisaliku.ee [2 C3]

This is probably the only restaurant in Tallinn that has the linguistic and gastronomic daring to have a website in French. It is quite right that they should, since this is provincial France transposed to medieval Tallinn. The frogs' legs on the menu prove the point. The tortuous stone steps leading down to the basement location are distinctly Estonian (or Scots) but then France takes over. Those who know 'Les Amis' in Vilnius will appreciate the need for a similar restaurant here. The menu is large enough to meet all tastes but small enough to ensure that mistakes are not made and that nothing synthetic is ever offered. The really greedy do not walk out onto Pikk immediately after eating here. They 'go to Belgium' upstairs at the café **Anneli Viik** for coffee and chocolate. *300EEK.*

✕ Spaghetteria Weizenbergi 18; ☎ 601 3636; www.restorankadriorg.ee [1 C2]

People-watching from restaurants in the town centre tends to involve horror at the misbehaving foreigners or concern for the rushing Estonians. The location of this restaurant, on a first floor above the tram stop for Kadriorg Park, gives views of a totally different kind. People who come here have time, and are relaxed. Raucous stag parties would never find their way here. Looking inwards is the kitchen, which forms the centre of this floor. The food is of course Italian, but it is perhaps significant that the wine list is much longer than the menu. Priorities here are clearly Italian too. *250EEK.*

✗ Teater Lai 31; ☎ 646 6261 [2 B2]

Coming into this basement from the stairs will often seem like an intrusion, so glued to their cigarettes and to TV are the staff and their close friends. However, walk through to a back alcove and the gathering will be interrupted to bring a mixed Creole and Estonian menu. Start with the grilled dishes from the former and finish with the pancakes from the latter. Do not expect any tender loving care here but the cheapness and the variety of the menu will be ample compensation. *200EEK.*

✗ Toomkooli Toomkooli 13; ☎ 644 6613; www.toomkooli.ee [3 A6]

Those who are not deterred by the awkward location at the back of the Old Town are rewarded on arrival with an extensive international menu and wine list but prices that have stayed Estonian. Minimal music and very heavy wooden chairs give a more formal air to the surroundings than is now common in many Tallinn restaurants, but in a town now so geared to the young, this should be taken as a compliment. *350EEK.*

✗ Vanaema Juures (Grandma's Place) Rataskaevu 10/12; ☎ 626 9080 [2 B4]

This is probably Tallinn's most famous restaurant but not even a visit from Hillary Clinton has gone to its head. The valid and repeated descriptions of it — good home cooking, traditional décor and a cosy atmosphere — degenerate into cliché but few would dispute them. The furnishings and photographs from the previous independence period (1918–40), together with discreet music from that time, deter the young and raucous, but others will immediately appreciate the originality of total Estonian surroundings. Unfortunately, Grandma has not got around yet to having a website. *300EEK.*

☕ CAFÉS AND BARS

There is little distinction between cafés and bars in Tallinn as no licences are needed to serve alcohol. Self-service at a counter remains common although practice varies as to whether clients then wait for the drinks or whether they are brought to the table. Those that open only in the evening are listed in *Chapter 7, Entertainment and Nightlife*. Those below are open all day and usually in the evening as well. Piped music is largely unavoidable but perhaps readers can help find a café where all music is banned so peace and quiet is assured. The success of those listed below should ensure that they are all still around during the currency of this book, although be prepared for name changes if a new owner takes over.

☕ Café Anglais

This section sadly has to start with an obituary rather than with a recommendation. Most of the expat community in Tallinn would come here regularly to pay local prices but to have a view over Town Hall Square. At the threat of closure, protests were as vigorous from the Quai d'Orsay as they were from Whitehall and Foggy Bottom, but all to no avail. The owners were not prepared to accept a rent which the café/restaurant could afford. At the time of writing (June 2006) it is still looking for premises whilst some of the staff have set up the Basso Lounge at Pikk 13.

☕ Déjà vu Sauna 1 [2 D4]

In English this sounds a derogatory name but to Estonians it suggests positive nostalgia. The red lights and orange stage recall the occasional glamorous nights out that were possible in Soviet times. The age of the clientele suggests that most of them were already going out in the 1980s and some now return at lunchtime if they are no longer up for flamboyant evenings. One page of the menu is surprisingly taken up just with tea, but the three pages covering all the alcoholic drinks makes up for this. Most of the staff are Russian-speaking but the variety of food available shows they must have travelled West quite frequently by now.

🍺 Elsebet Viru 2 [2 C4]

Lunch on the run is not yet a Tallinn phenomenon, despite the serious business environment. However, those who want to bring London practice with them can race into the ground floor here and will be out in 5mins at most with a range of sandwiches, quiches and cakes. The more sensible visitor will forget breakfast in the hotel for once to arrive here with a camera at 08.00 so that a window table on the first floor will be theirs. Stay for a couple of hours to see the last of yesterday's drunks being picked up, the Tallinn élite coming out of their expensive flats and the first of the cruise parties meandering towards Town Hall Square. Don't forget a zoom lens to catch unsuspecting faces and Tallinn's windows and roofs.

🍷 Gloria Veinikelder Müürivahe 2; www.gloria.ee [3 D6]

It seems a shame to ignore Estonia whilst in Tallinn but that is what anyone who comes here has to do. Forget vodka or the local Vana Tallinn and concentrate on the 2,000 different bottles not only of wine but also of cognac and whiskey. Many foreigners justify their presence in this wine bar by pointing out that they can enjoy their 'own' drinks here at prices much lower than those charged at home. That the bar is called 'Napoleon' shows where most of these 2,000 bottles come from.

♀ **IceBar** Dunkri 4–6; www icebar.ee [2 C4]

Super cool bar in the Merchant House Hotel. Sample a vodka from a glass moulded from ice or choose from the extensive range of delicious cocktails on offer.

♀ **Kaheksa** Vana-Posti 8; entrance from Müürivahe [3 D5]

Kaheksa means 'eight' but nobody seems to know the reason for this name. The austere granite Sõprus Cinema to which this is an adjunct is a surprising backcloth but indoors a totally tropical environment is created. The décor is light, as are the drinks, most of which are rum and coconut based. Teetotallers can hide their abstinence behind fruit-smoothies which are really light desserts. From about 2002, a Caribbean theme hit Tallinn and here it is at its best. Perhaps a visit here in midwinter is inadvisable as leaving will be a blow; wait until the summer when the outside will from time to time rival the interior. Given its proximity to Hollywood, one of Tallinn's largest nightclubs, the clientele here is inevitably young, particularly in the early evening.

☕ **Kohvicum** Uus 16 [2 D3]

This is in the basement of the Music Academy (Muusikamaja), but is open to the public. Its warmth is welcome in winter and so is the opposite in summer. It is run by the Kehrwieder group who own a number of dependable cafés around Tallinn. The location is most useful, given the few other cafés in this part of the Old Town. The Kehrwieder website (*www.kohvik.ee*) gives a full list of their cafés and their locations.

☕ **Maiasmokk** Pikk 16 [2 C3]

It is nice to find a café that is unashamedly old-fashioned. The panelling is dark, the staff middle aged and the food prepared on the spot. It is provincial in the best sense of the word, being one of the very few cafés in Tallinn that are spared piped music. Prices also stay two or three years behind those charged elsewhere, particularly surprising given its location on the tourist beat in the centre of the Old Town. There is a separate entrance to the restaurant, which consists of small dining rooms on the first floor that can be booked for private groups of 8 to 10. Choose the view carefully: one overlooks the balcony of the Russian Embassy from which the occupation of Estonia was proclaimed in 1940. In summer 2004, the Kalev Chocolate Museum moved to the top floor of the restaurant, but even by summer 2006 had not completely reopened.

☐P Meistrite Hoov (Masters' Courtyard) Vene 6 [2 C4]

Whilst gentrification continues apace through most of Tallinn's Old Town, it is pleasant still to find a quarter that remains genuinely bohemian. Lavish chocolates are usually expected in boutiques or at least in department stores. Here, too, they are available, and in fact are the main attraction in a café called **Chocolaterie** where suits are unknown, where self-service is the norm and where soft cushions cover the chairs. Expect to be surrounded by modern art, both in painting and in ceramics. The size of the exhibition depends on the weather; it rapidly expands outdoors whenever it can.

☐P Mini-many Maakri 22 [1 A3]

This wooden house could not be a greater contrast to the Radisson Hotel on the other side of the road. It has only 5 tables and serves plain home cooking on traditional black-and-white tablecloths. The clientele is largely local but the occasional foreigner is now seen here.

☐P Mocha Vene 1 [2 C4]

Return visitors to Tallinn will remember this as the Mary and there seems little need for a name change. The selection of teas remains as extensive as that of the coffees and for those who would be happier in Austria or Germany, the Mocha provides perfect solace. After a cake or two here there is no need for lunch or supper. Papers to read abound, there is no rush and the music is much quieter than elsewhere. The neighbouring shops change frequently; let us hope that Mocha sees no need to follow suit. The Irish and Italian embassies share a building over the road so their flags plus the EU one make the café easy to find.

🖵🍵 Moskva Vabaduse Väljak 10; 📞 640 4694; www.moskva.ee [3 D6]
Some cafés survive in Tallinn on sheer cheek and this must be one of them. The name is as risky as ever given the poisonous level of relations with Russia, and the location of this café on Freedom Square. The décor remains gloomy and the website is in dark brown, with no foreign-language translations. Yet local expats and Estonians return again and again. Perhaps it is for a sense of security as much as for the 1990s prices. The food will always be dependable, as is the company; the music, if noticeable at all, will not intrude.

🍷 Musi (Kiss) Niguliste 6; 📞 644 3100; www.musi.ee [3 C5]
This wine bar opened almost without anybody noticing in spring 2005. As it is situated on one of the main tourist routes, it is perhaps just as well, so tourists who do track it down will be rewarded with suburban prices and an almost homely feel, so small are the rooms. The entrance is through two sets of stiff wooden doors. The abstemious will be able to have a meal here from the salads and pies on offer and nobody need worry about being over 25. It is probably a good sign, if a surprising one, that 9 months after opening, the menu and the website are still only in Estonian. Foreigners are welcome, but they must fit in.

🖵🍵 Otto's Pikk 35 [2 C3]
For the moment cafés are few and far between on Pikk, although it is a central street in the Old Town. Although the décor here is modern, this one generally attracts an older clientele who are rewarded with lower

prices and larger portions than those usually offered elsewhere. They may also prefer the smaller size as there are only 5 tables.

🖥 **Põllu** Rävala 8 [1 A3]
The headquarters of the Estonian Civil Aviation Administration, close to the Radisson and Viru hotels, is an unusual place to look for coffee but for those on a tight budget and not the least interested in atmosphere, the public café in the basement rewards those who track it down, with coffee for 4EEK (16p/27c), light snacks for 12EEK (50p/70c) and hot meals for around 22EEK (£1/US$1.60). The hot dishes come straight from the freezer and the flowers on the tables are guaranteed to be artificial, but at these prices who should care?

🖥 **Scotland Yard** Mere pst 6e; ✆ 653 5190; www.scotlandyard.ee [2 D1]
Many British antique shops must have been plundered to recreate the 1890s here, though whether gunsmiths needed to relinquish so much of their old stock is a moot point. The guns worn by the staff are fortunately fakes. Proximity to the port attracts the wilder, rougher crowd on Fri and Sat nights, but more conventional guests will feel happy here during the day and might even want to stay for a meal. Despite the old-fashioned décor, it is very much a young set who come here.

🍸 **Stereo Lounge** Harju 6; ✆ 631 0549; www.stereolounge.ee [3 D6]
Older visitors will remember **George Browne's** that used to be at this address. While pubs remained a novelty in Tallinn, its formula worked, but Stereo has shown that by 2004 a change was very necessary. The décor is totally white here, except for the staff who are in easyJet orange and the bottles which have

stayed as their manufacturers produced them. There is no longer any need to battle to the bar for a drink; it and a healthy range of light dishes can quickly be brought to any table, but for those able to support themselves on a bar stool, the array of drinks served and the breadth of the TV screen will provide an enticing vista.

♀ **Tapas & Vino** Suur Karja 4; ✆ 631 3232 [3 D5]
Suur Karja is notorious for the number of bars on it catering only to loud-mouthed stag parties. It was courageous for a serious wine bar to open here early in 2005 but the gamble has paid off. The cracks in the ceiling beams and the Soviet dark-brown panelling under the bar cleverly deters those who would not be welcome. The pile of Estonian literary journals, laid ready for customers at the entrance, is probably a further no-no to such people. The middle aged, those who like to talk, or the experimenters willing to try Israeli wine or Canadian whiskey will doubtless linger here. Maybe the tapas can soon be enlarged into full meals and a stay in one of the deep armchairs extended from one hour to two.

💻 **Tristan ja Isolde** Raekoja Plats 1 [2 C4]
Although part of the Town Hall, its entrance is so well concealed that, even at the height of the tourist season, space is often available. However, the most enticing time to come is in midwinter late in the evening. Stride across the deserted snow-covered square, pull open the squeaking door and enjoy *glühwein* in what looks like a Swiss country inn. Follow this with Irish coffee and chocolate cake and hopefully the warmth will last until you get back to your hotel.

7 Entertainment and Nightlife

On regaining independence, Tallinn started to rebel against the limited and formal entertainment that had previously been available. Out went dance bands, string quartets and folk dancing; in came discotheques, striptease and jazz. Private enterprise immediately seized the Finnish market that came every weekend laden with money and determined to spend it – not necessarily in the most sensible of ways; vodka at a quarter of the price it is at home is bound to lead to grief. Above all, the night went on until breakfast. No club now dares to close before 02.00. Admission fees are rare so it is common to sample quite a few different places in one evening. Now that Tallinn has a large middle class, the clientele is very mixed in most clubs as Estonians no longer feel excluded from them. None is yet typecast but go for smart-casual dress. Anything torn or ill-fitting is frowned on in Estonia. Better to be out of date than out of figure.

Before the clubs open, rock and pop concerts draw large crowds to **Linnahall**, near the harbour. It has performances most evenings.

OPERA, CONCERTS AND CINEMA

The Estonian National Opera (*www.opera.ee*) [3 A5] has performances three or four times a week. Specialist tour operators can pre-book tickets as the programme is fixed about six months in advance. Given the inevitable government cutbacks in this field, it is remarkable how up to date the building now is following its 1998–2005 reconstruction, with the stage lighting being particularly impressive. Unlike Riga, Estonia's opera rarely attracts world-famous performers – and indeed some Estonian performers, especially in this field, have been attracted abroad by the much higher fees paid there. But the fact that about 30% of the opera's tickets year-round are sold to non-Estonians shows the high standard that it offers, as well as the very reasonable prices charged. Even after the Opera House reopened in December 2005 following its restoration, the highest ticket price was usually 300EEK (£13/US$20) and many cost much less. Performances are always in the original language; 20% or so are of contemporary Estonian works, the remainder are popular classics. The opera is closed in July and August.

Classical concerts are held in the **Old Town Hall** [2 C4], the **Estonia Concert Hall** [3 A5], the **House of Blackheads** [2 C3] and in **St Nicholas's Church** [3 C5], all of these venues being in the Old Town. In the summer of 2006, the new art gallery **KUMU** [1 D3] also started a concert programme. In most cases tickets are sold only on the day or the day before the concert so there is no need (or possibility) to pre-book from abroad. Whilst some performances take place in midsummer, music lovers are well advised to come at other times of year when the choice and standard is far higher. The website (*www.festivals.ee*) gives the full range of music festivals held throughout Estonia each year. There is not a regular pattern, and many of these take place in Tallinn, with an increasing number annually.

Young people congregate at **Linnahall** [1 A1], the concert hall beside the heliport near the harbour, where live music is staged most evenings. Performers are always local. Sometimes this is replaced by family shows and sometimes by raucous Russian plays not genteel enough for the main Russian Theatre. The website (*www.linnahall.ee*) is only in Estonian (*Pileti hind* are the ticket prices and *Jäähalli* is the ice-skating rink).

Films are always subtitled and never dubbed so tourists can see films missed at home without any problem. The **Sõprus** Cinema (*www.kino.ee*) [3 D5] in the Old Town at Vana-Posti 8 is easily accessible from many hotels. Younger people now flock to **Coca-Cola Plaza** (*www.superkinod.ee*) [1 A2], a combination of 11 separate cinemas and a shopping mall. It is situated behind the Central Post Office on Viru Square and so is also close to many hotels.

NIGHTLIFE

Tallinn prides itself on its nightlife and some tour operators promote it extensively. It does tend to attract some people who should really have kept their vomiting and urinating back home in Britain and Finland. As a major stag destination from 2003, perhaps it will finally fall from popularity in 2006 when these crowds move elsewhere.

Fortunately, nightclubs do not go in and out of favour as quickly in Tallinn as they do elsewhere and many clubs that were thriving six or seven years ago still thrive now. Many do not charge an entrance fee, particularly midweek, so if you find you have stumbled into somewhere not to your taste, it won't cost much to move on.

The clubs listed below are all totally different, and this is deliberate. *Tallinn In Your Pocket* keeps very up to date on this topic as it is published six times a year and not being dependent on advertising can be objective. To whet your appetite, check their website (*www.inyourpocket.com*) before leaving home.

☆ **Bonnie & Clyde** Olümpia Hotel, Liivalaia 33 [1 A3]
As this club is safely ensconced in a 4-star hotel, it is never a mistake to suggest a date here. Do, however, dress up properly, firstly to get in and secondly not to lower the tone. If you are under 25, you may well not want to try unless you can be sure of being taken for at least 30. If you are 45, do not worry. Nearly everybody else is too. This was the venue chosen by 53-year-old Toomas Hendrik Ilves to celebrate his presidential victory in September 2006.

☆ **Eiffel** Grand Hotel, Toompuiestee 27 [3 A7]
The hotel caters for staid, elderly tourist groups wanting a quiet base near the Old Town, but this rooftop club is far more broad-minded, both in its music and in its clientele. The music is normally live, which makes the volume sensible for those wanting to be able to talk with their guests. The view up to the floodlit Tall Hermann Tower is a pleasant contrast to the cellar walls on offer in so many other clubs, as

is the space to move around. Smart-casual dress is the norm, though extremes in either direction can sometimes be seen.

☆ Harley Davidson Dunkri 11 [2 C4]
This club must clearly be a rebellion against the deluxe St Petersbourg Hotel on the other side of the road. Nobody here has any dress sense at all and if they cannot arrive on a motorbike, will certainly not choose a taxi instead. Pretend to be under 25 to be comfortable here and, yes, a leather jacket is the common currency. Probably to stop endless protests from hotel grandees, the club closes at midnight during the week and at the comparatively early time of 02.00 on Fri and Sat nights.

☆ La Casa del Habano Dunkri 2 [2 C4]
For those who hate nightlife but for business reasons have to pretend otherwise, Tallinn's first cigar lounge provided the perfect answer. To impress, insist on a Cuban cigar, but the miserly can also order Danish and Dutch ones. Sit at the window during the evening and see all of single Tallinn go by, some to the St Petersbourg Hotel and some to the Harley Davidson described above. As the lounge is also open during the day, come back then for a different view of families and cruise passengers.

☆ Molly Malone's Mündi 2 [2 C4]
Yes, the old aluminium Guinness advertisements are corny, yes the music can be dated and yes, because of the location on Town Hall Square it can get very crowded in summer, but nonetheless a visit to Tallinn is not complete without a look-in at Molly's. Expats regularly congregated here, even before fish and chips came onto the menu. In the summer, spilling onto the square is normal so relative peace can alternate with Irish liveliness.

GAY TALLINN

Given Tallinn's devotion to anything Western, it is rather surprising how limited the gay scene is. Whilst the legal restraints they faced in Soviet times have all of course been abolished, the hostility the gay community then faced has still not been eradicated. As a result, open affection outside the few gay clubs is very unusual and visitors are advised to avoid this. Some clubs even function behind closed doors and it is necessary to ring a bell to gain admission. Opening hours can often change, as can nights on which women are admitted. This should be checked on their websites.

A gay pride week has taken place in Tallinn each August since 2004, helping to increase tolerance and understanding amongst the general community. The website www.pride.ee not only gives the programme for these celebrations, but also covers the gay scene in Tallinn overall.

Three well-established clubs are:

☆ **Club Angel** Sauna 1; www.clubangel.ee [2 D4]
The opening of this club, situated in the heart of the Old Town, in late 2004 can perhaps be taken as the start of a more tolerant approach to the gay community. There is nothing discreet about the contents of the website or at the entrance. It is open three nights a week, Thu–Sat, but during the day and on other evenings there is a café where all are welcome.

☆ **Ring Club** Juhkentali 11; www.ringclub.ee [1 B4]
Women and striptease are strictly segregated here but do check the explicit and detailed English-language website before setting off. Juhkentali is close to the bus station and is hardly the most salubrious road in Tallinn, which perhaps suits the risqué approach of this club and the gloomy underground surroundings in which its activities take place.

☆ **X-Baar** Sauna 1; www.zone.ee/xbaar [2 D4]
With its central location, comparatively long history and small size, this is probably the place to go first in Tallinn. The jazz and the pink décor will provide reassuring surroundings.

8 Shopping

From Monday to Friday most shops open 10.00–18.00 and on Saturday they close earlier, usually around 16.00. On Sunday they stay closed. However, those in the Old Town of interest to tourists open in the summer 10.00–19.00 seven days a week. Supermarkets open seven days a week, usually 09.00–21.00. It is now rare to find a shop that does not accept credit cards although they are not, of course, of use in the markets. There is one all-night shop in the Old Town, Kolm Jalg at Pikk 3 [2 B4] and another just outside it, Westmani at Pärnu 19 [3 A7].

BOOKS AND POSTCARDS

Postcards are best bought at the post office beside the Alexander Nevsky Cathedral at the top of Toompea. It has a wide selection and they usually cost half the price charged by the rather pushy street sellers who now crowd the Old Town. Philatelists will find a good selection of stamps here.

Apollo Viru 23; www.apollo.ee [2 E3]
This is Tallinn's first book and map shop largely geared to the expat community and the tourists walking past

from the harbour into the Old Town. The windows have an extensive display of tourist literature, everything is labelled in English and there is a quiet café, almost hidden, in a corner of the first floor. It also stocks maps and guides to the surrounding Baltic countries, including a good selection of Bradt ones. Perhaps wisely, it has closed the ramshackle antiquarian section that used to be attached. If you have run out of reading matter, this is the place to stock up. English-language paperbacks cost roughly the same as in the UK.

Huma Vene 14; www.huma.ee [2 C3]
Publishes many of the postcards sold around the Old Town as well as some of the booklets and calendars, so anyone willing to climb to their third-floor office will be rewarded with lower prices than those on the street. Their website shows every postcard they have.

Juhan Hammer Roosikrantsi 6; www.oldbooks.ee [3 E7]
This is the least disorganised of Tallinn's many secondhand bookshops for those who succeed in finding it open. Most foreigners come here to find something unexpected from home, rather than anything on Estonia, but the collection of old Estonian postcards is always thorough. There is usually a range of books in English from the Soviet period and some too from the 1920–40 independence period.

Raamatukoi Harju 1, just below St Nicholas's Church; www.raamatukoi.ee [3 D5]
For several years, this was the bookshop Felix and Fabian, but fortunately when they closed early in 2006, Raamatukoi were happy to leave their premises next to Apollo on Viru and take these ones up. The Writers Union, who own the building, were firm that Tallinn should not be plagued with yet another fashion shop. The location is ideal for tourists, being so close to Town Hall Square and opposite the tourist office. They have an

up-to-date and reasonably priced selection of tourist books in foreign languages, postcards, as well as a secondhand section with mainly books from Soviet times. Quite a number of these are in English and many are well illustrated, so the photographs can to some extent compensate for a text now largely unacceptable.

Rahva Raamat Pärnu mnt 10 [3 E6]
Probably Tallinn's most famous bookshop. Its extensive secondhand section is a treasure-trove of works on art and architecture, many totally in English or with at least an English summary in them. The premises became 'threatened' by Hugo Boss in autumn 2003 who were eager to purchase some of the current shop as an outlet for their clothes and could of course offer a much higher rent than a bookshop could pay. The wave of protests to which this gave rise, led by Estonia's most famous writer Jaan Kross, was not in the end successful and visitors from 2004 onwards have had to make do with a much smaller bookshop here as a result.

SOUVENIRS

A one-stop shop for souvenirs, since it stocks linen, woollen jerseys, ceramics and wooden toys, is **Puupood** at Lai 5 [2 B4] and although in the Old Town, it is just off the main tourist circuit so prices are very reasonable. A similarly diverse range can be found at **Madeli Käsitöö** at Väike-Karja 1 [2 D4], where a walk from the Town Hall Square of two–three minutes will likewise be rewarded with considerably lower prices.

A walk along **Katariina Käik** between Vene and Müürivahe [2 D3] will satisfy even the most fastidious shopper. This lane is lined with workshops covering every form of applied art, so tourists with time can order an item of clothing or jewellery specifically to their taste. Turn right into Müürivahe for the **Wall of Sweaters** [2 D4]. Whether the temperature is 30°F or 30°C, the stock here is always the same, geared totally to the needs of an Estonian winter. By also buying socks, gloves and fur hats, visitors are granted complete protection against it.

Serious competition for Katariina Käik began to emerge at **Meistrite Hoov** (Masters' Courtyard) at Vene 6 [2 C4] during 2006, when restoration finally started in earnest, after ten years of occasional outbursts. The project should be complete by 2007. It is a condition of renting premises in this former rabbit warren or workshops and small houses that only Estonian goods are sold. It would normally be hard to justify ethnic cleansing, but here it is fully justified. There is nothing wrong with Russian dolls, Lithuanian amber or Chinese paper-cuts, but Tallinn Old Town should not be the place to promote them.

Helina Tilk, Rataskaevu 6 [2 B4] has probably the largest selection of locally produced china and glassware. Very little of their work has pictures of Tallinn on it since the aim is to represent local art, not to provide mantelpiece dust collectors.

For those who can restrict themselves to wooden dolls, **Nukupood** on Town Hall Square (Raekoja Plats 18) [2 C4] is conveniently located and has an enormous choice. **Kaubamaja** is Tallinn's largest department store and is situated halfway between the

Viru and Radisson hotels at Gonsiori 2 [1 A3]. It will supply any forgotten toiletry article or item of clothing and is worth visiting for its CDs of Estonian music and for its porcelain. Take the outside lift to look down on the redevelopment of Viru Square, which includes a shopping complex now linked both to the hotel of the same name and to Kaubamaja. It is quite expensive, but the range is convenient and being completely enclosed, the weather is irrelevant. Its multilingual website (*www.virukeskus.com*) gives full details of all the shops that it includes. **Stockmann** is the department store where all successful Estonians like to be seen doing their shopping. It is a branch of Helsinki's most famous department store. One outlet is attached to the Viru Hotel [1 A3] and the main shop is next to the Olümpia Hotel, at Liivalaia 53.

In midsummer an arts and crafts market stretches across **Raekoja Plats** (Town Hall Square) [2 C4]. Do, however, watch out for pickpockets here since this is their favourite haunt. To see where local people not yet seduced by supermarkets do their daily shopping, visit **Keskturg** (Central Market), ironically only about 200m from Stockmann, just off the Tartu road [1 C4].

Do not expect any of the elegance of Riga market here; it in fact only got a roof in 2003 so down to earth is probably the best description of it, particularly as much of the trade is in fruit and vegetables. Some Finns come for spare parts for their cars, basic linen goods and pirate CDs.

Those who shop for necessity rather than for pleasure usually call in at the hypermarket **Ülemiste** (*www.ulemiste.ee* [1 C4]), beside the hotel of the same name a few hundred yards from the airport. It sells a wide range of souvenirs, cheap household goods, black bread and vodka which can be picked up just before checking in for a flight. The number 2 bus stops here en route to town and to the airport. There are plans to make what is currently the car park into a major transport complex with a bus station, railway station and the airport all together.

FOOD AND DRINK

As Estonia's entry into the European Union has allowed visitors from other member states to bring home virtually all the drink and tobacco they can take in their luggage, it is worthwhile looking around at the prices different shops charge for these goods. (See page 105 for some restrictions on cigarettes.) Avoid the ones by the harbour as they are frequented by desperate Finns who will pay anything as long as it is less than in Helsinki. Buy the local vodka and the aperitif Vana Tallinn as savings will be greater here than on imported goods.

The **Rimi** supermarket at Aia 7 (*open daily 09.00–21.00*) [2 D3] is the best source of picnic supplies and provisions for self-caterers. Nowhere is the demise of the USSR clearer than here as the selection is mostly American rather than European. The provision of free coffee by the cakes counter is a clever marketing device to ensure visitors linger longer and buy more. The shop also has an extensive soft and alcoholic drinks section.

Also in Aia, at 5b next to the Tavid foreign exchange bureau, is **Bakhos** (*open daily 08.00–21.00*) [2 D3], which is one of the cheapest sources of drink in Tallinn. **Araxis**

[2 E3] in the Old Fire Station on Viru Square is another popular source for drink, partly because it used to be open 24 hours a day (but changes in the law now force it to close at 23.00). **Ararat**, next to the bookshop Apollo in Viru, also closes at 23.00.

Cigarettes are best bought by the carton rather than by the packet. Costs vary quite considerably from kiosk to kiosk so it is worth looking around outside the Old Town where prices are invariably lower than within it. British visitors should note that despite Estonia's entry into the EU, the cigarette allowance on returning home is still only one carton – 200 cigarettes.

Kalev, Estonia's famous chocolate producer, has a shop at Lai 1 [2 B4] near the centre of the Old Town with good prices, but chocoholics should also check the new location of their museum above Maiasmokk café at Pikk 16.

9 Walking Tours

Tourists tend to concentrate on the Old Town but many modern buildings are of interest too. While the main sights in the Old Town can be covered in one day, more time is needed for other sights. A route for a day-long walking tour is suggested followed by some other shorter ones.

WALK ONE

Start at the final Soviet architectural legacy to Estonia, the **National Library** (Eesti Rahvusraamatukogu), begun in 1986 and completed in 1993 (see page 140 [3 C8]). It is situated on the intersection of Endla and Tõnismägi close to the Mihkli and Santa Barbara hotels.

Cross the road to **Charles's Church** (Kaarli kirik). With its almost Episcopalian simplicity it is the perfect antidote to what is to come later in the walk (see page 150 [3 C8]). On leaving the church, turn right into Kaarli and then take the first road on the left, Toompea. The **Occupation Museum** opened here in summer 2003 (see page 142 [3 C7]).

Continuing up the hill, at the first crossroads, note the simple monument to 20

August 1991, the date Estonia declared independence during the
failed Moscow coup. Had it been necessary, Estonians were
ready to use the walls and towers to defend the Old Town from
possible Soviet attack but the quick collapse of the coup and the
immediate recognition by the USSR of Estonian independence
prevented this. Looking ahead is a monument that dates from
the 15th century, **Pikk Hermann** (Tall Hermann Tower [3B6]).
It has withstood numerous invasions and remains intact. Its
height of nearly 50m is supported by foundations 15m deep.
The first Estonian flag was flown from here in 1884, 34 years
before the country was to become independent. Subsequent
conquerors always marked their success by raising a flag here.
A German guidebook printed in 1942 lists 12 major dates in
Tallinn's history, the last being 28 August 1941, when the German flag
was raised over Pikk Hermann. On 20 September 1944 the Estonian flag was raised
as the Germans were leaving, but the Germans were still able to insist that their flag
should fly together with the Estonian one on 21 September. Both had gone by the
following day, when the Soviet forces seized Tallinn. During the Soviet occupation,
the Estonian SSR flag was flown, but the Estonian national flag returned in 1989. It is
raised at sunrise and lowered at sunset, except at midsummer when it is not lowered
at all on the night of June 23/24. The blue in the flag represents the sky, black the soil,
and white the aspirations of the Estonian people.

Tall Hermann Tower

Turn right down the hill (Komandandi) to **Kiek in de Kök** ('Peep in the Kitchen', see page 138 [3 C6]). The reason for the name becomes obvious as one climbs the 45m tower to the sixth floor and peers into more and more houses; only the steeples of St Nicholas and St Olav are higher. Kiek in de Kök does not have any catering but the nearest tower to it, **Megedi**, can be recommended in this respect. This tower, like most in the city wall, dates from the late 14th century and was continually enlarged during the 15th century. From around 1800 when its defensive potential declined, it was converted into a barracks. In 1980, the top floor became a café which uses the name Megedi, and the ground floor a restaurant, called Neitsitorn.

On leaving Kiek in de Kök turn back up the hill and turn right into Toompea, which ends in the square between **Parliament** (Riigikogu, see page 143 [3 B6]) and the **Alexander Nevsky Cathedral** (see page 150 [3 B6]). The juxtaposition of these

Toompea

two buildings appropriately contrasts official Estonian and Russian architecture. The one is simple, small and functional, the other elaborate and deliberately powerful, a completely Russian architectural outpost dominating the Tallinn skyline. The **Parliament Building**, the interior of which dates from 1921, is one of very few in the Old Town to have seen frequent reconstruction, the last one resulting from a fire in 1917 which may have been started by the Bolsheviks.

Continue up the hill along Toomkooli with the post office on your right. By the end of 2006, this street should be completely restored, the first one to be back to its 1920s glory. Straight ahead, on Kiriku Square, is the **Dome Church** (Toomkirik), sometimes called St Mary's Cathedral (see page 151 [3 B5]).

As you turn left out of the church, the **Estonian Knighthood Building** dominates the opposite side of Kiriku Square. From 1992 until 2006 it provided temporary shelter for the Estonian Art Museum that now has its own building in Kadriorg. Turning sharp right from the museum along Toom Rüütli leads, after 150m, to the main viewpoint across Tallinn. It is inevitably crowded during the tourist season so an alternative can be recommended along Rahukohtu, on the corner of Rüütli. Rahukohtu also starts on the right-hand side of the gallery. To reach the lower town, it is necessary in either case to return along Piiskopi towards the Russian cathedral and then to walk down the steps of Lühike Jalg ('Short Leg'), rather a misnomer as there are in fact about 100 steps. At the top, though, are several tempting cafés, souvenir shops and well-maintained toilets which can provide a respite before continuing the walk. Before starting the descent, look to the left along Pikk Jalg ('Long Leg'). The façade which commands one of the best views over Tallinn is modelled on the main building of Tartu University. Perhaps appropriately, in view of the current strength of the Estonian economy, this imposing building houses the Ministry of Finance. On the right at the end of Lühike Jalg is the

Adamson-Eric Museum (see page 124 [3 C5]).

Continuing down the hill, the steps become a road which continues to a junction. To the left is Rataskaevu and to the right, Rüütli, both roads which house some of Tallinn's most famous restaurants. Ahead is **Niguliste** (St Nicholas's Church, see page 153 [3 C6]), which, like many other early churches in Tallinn, was a military installation as well as a church, with ample hiding places and secret exits to the city walls. Coming out of the church and turning left along Rüütli, the next building on the left is the Swedish **Church of St Michael** (see page 153 [3 C6]).

On leaving the church, turn right to the memorial to the writer **Eduard Vilde** (1865–1933). The illustrations depict scenes from his novels and plays, and the two stones represent an open book. Between 1918 and 1920 he served as Estonian ambassador in Copenhagen and Berlin, convincing both governments that an independent Estonia was here to stay. The **Tallinn Tourist Information Centre** (see page 47 [3 C5]) is on the other side of the road. Proceed down the steps to Harju. Ahead is the bookshop Raamatukoi, but on the corner of Harju and Kuninga note the plaque to the writer Juhan Smuul (1922–71) who lived here as the building belongs to the Writers Union. Despite winning both Stalin and Lenin prizes and being chairman of the Writers Union, he was a genuinely popular writer at the time which is why the plaque has not been removed. Hopefully, his works will soon be republished. Jaan Kross (born 1920), Estonia's most famous contemporary writer, still lives in this complex and is fit enough to reach his fourth-floor flat without a lift. (In Soviet times, only buildings with five floors or more had lifts installed.)

Turn into Harju. The bombed site on the right has deliberately been left as it was, following the bombing raid of 9 March 1944. The inscription commemorates the 463 people killed that night. In June 2002, a referendum was held in Tallinn about the future of this site. Only 2% of the population turned out to vote, but 87% of them wanted to keep the site as a memorial and not let it fall into the hands of developers. In 2006 the area was bought by the town council for 150 milllion kroon (£6 million/US$11 million). It is a sum that inevitably gave rise to controversy, but it will ensure that the area is maintained as a permanent memorial.

Returning along Harju and then Kullassepa brings one into **Raekoja Plats**, or Town Hall Square [2 C4]. Just before reaching the square, it is worth turning right for a few minutes into the small alley, Raekoja. The building on the right, which now houses the **Photographic Museum** (see page 145), was the town's main prison until the early 19th century.

Town
Hall

The Town Hall Square is similar to many in northern Germany as it was the commercial centre for the Baltic Germans. In the 16th century, the Germans accounted for about 1,500 of Tallinn's total population of around 5,000. They maintained all positions of authority, ruling from the Town Hall and the surrounding buildings. The square was the centre for all major events in the town, happy and tragic. Carnivals, weddings and Christmas have all been regularly celebrated here and the Tallinn Old Days

Festival, held each year in early June, recreates the carnival atmosphere with its musical and artistic events. What was probably the world's first Christmas tree was displayed here in 1441. Yet the square was also the site for frequent executions and floggings, its grimmest day being in 1806 when 72 peasants were executed following a failed uprising. Nowadays it is hard to imagine such a background as work and punishment have given way to total relaxation. Cafés surround the square and spread into it during the summer. Since 2001, a Christmas market has taken place here throughout December. One of the few buildings on the square that has kept its original function is the **Pharmacy** (see page 144 [2 C4]), which dates from 1422. The **Town Hall** (see page 148 [2 C4]) is the only late Gothic building still intact in Estonia, dating largely from the 15th century.

Across the square, opposite the Town Hall, are several short streets which lead to Pikk. On the corner of Mündi and Town Hall Square is a millennium clock which counted down the seconds until midnight on 31 December 1999. Saiakäik is the smallest street in Tallinn. Take either Mündi or Saiakäik and turn right to the junction of Pikk and Pühavaimu for the **Holy Ghost Church** (Pühavaimu, see page 152 [2 C4]). Cross Pikk for the **Estonian History Museum** (Ajaloomuuseum, see page 132 [2 C4]), whose building is as impressive as any of the contents, perhaps more so. As you turn left into Pikk, the new Russian Embassy is on the left and on the right is Maiasmokk, a café that has deliberately stayed old-fashioned both in décor and in prices. The name translates appropriately as 'sweet tooth'. In summer 2004, the **Kalev Chocolate Museum** moved here too (see page 136 [2 C3]), but in 2006 some of its exhibits still remained to be displayed. Pikk has two of the few notable Jugendstil or Art Nouveau buildings in Tallinn, both designed by Jacques Rosenbaum. Number 18, next to Maiasmokk, has a flamboyant Egyptian theme; number 25 on the corner of Hobusepea is more modest. Number 61, built across Pagari, and probably the blandest building in the Old Town, was the KGB headquarters in Soviet times and now houses the Interior Ministry. Unlike its opposite number in Vilnius, it has not been opened to the public.

Next on the left is **St Olav's Church** (Oleviste, see page 155 [2 C2]), named after the king of Norway and now a Baptist church. A few yards further down on the right is **Fat Margaret's Tower** which houses the **Maritime Museum** (Meremuuseum, see page 139 [2 C1]). Outside is a plaque unveiled by Prince Andrew in May 1998 which commemorates British naval involvement in the battles between Estonian forces and the Bolsheviks from 1918 to 1920.

Turn right out of the museum and leave the Old Town on Suur Rannavärara, the continuation of Pikk. On the right is the monument to those who died in the *Estonia* tragedy in 1994. It can be interpreted in a number of ways, perhaps symbolising the boat breaking into two or the total divide between life and death. Cross Põhja puiestee to the disused power station, now ironically the **Energy Museum** (Energeetikamuuseum, see page 128). Built originally in the late 1920s, it then had some claim to Jugendstil influence but many subsequent alterations have completely removed any hint of beauty and style.

Return into the Old Town and walk behind Fat Margaret along Uus. Number 37 is the **Marine Mine Museum** [2 C1] which opened in 2003. The mines displayed here (and the objects made out of them) all come from Naissaar Island (see page 173) off the coast from Tallinn, which was the centre of production for the whole of the Soviet Union. Number 31 is the **Scottish Club** [2 C4], in fact a restaurant open to all. It has the best-maintained lawn in Estonia. Next door is a whiskey shop, a clear testimony to Tallinn's affluence and passion for Western consumer goods. It is hard to believe that until 1989 whiskey was available only in foreign currency shops. Turn right into Olevimägi and then left into Vene. On the left is a smaller, but no less Russian version of the Alexander Nevsky Cathedral, **St Nicholas's Russian Orthodox Church** [2 C3]. Again no concessions are made to Estonia; everything is written, spoken and sung in Russian. It dates from the early 19th century. On the right at number 17 is the **City Museum** (Linnamuuseum, see page 126 [2 C3]). As with the History Museum, the building is as of much interest as the contents. Having escaped the fires that ravished so many buildings in the Old Town, this 14th-century merchant's house still has examples of 16th-century wooden panelling, windows and furniture.

On the left are the ruins of the **Dominican Monastery** [2 D3], founded in 1246 but destroyed during the Reformation in 1524 when the monks were forced to flee. Extensive archaeological excavations were carried out between 1954 and 1968 when the ruins were first opened to the public. Take a torch and wear sturdy shoes as the surviving ambulatories are poorly lit. Of most interest are the stone carvings by the 16th-century Dutch sculptor Arent Passer. Chamber-music concerts take place here during the summer. On leaving the monastery, turn left into Vene and left again into **Katariina Käik** [2 D3]. Gravestones from the monastery are lined up along the left-hand wall. This tiny alleyway is where local expats buy their souvenirs of Tallinn, as few tourists find it. It is also used as a film set. Turn right at the end into Müürivahe, which runs below the city walls. Elderly Russians have stalls here, selling woollen sweaters, gloves and socks both in midsummer and in midwinter. The walk ends at the junction with Viru Street. To the left is the 15th-century **Viru Gate** [2 D4], as formidable as the fortifications seen at the start of the walk. To the right is McDonald's; will it also last five centuries?

Visitors with more time can see many museums in addition to those mentioned in the walk. Close to the Viru Gate at Vana Viru 14 and opposite the Viru Hotel is the **Fire-Fighting Museum** (see page 183 [2 E3]). Back in the Old Town, in Lai, are the **Applied Arts Museum** (see page 125 [2 B3]) at number 17 and the **Health Museum** (see page 132 [2 B3]) at numbers 28–30.

Next to the Applied Arts Museum is the **Natural History Museum** (see page 142 [2 B2]) at Lai 29, and then the **Theatre and Music Museum** (see page 147 [3 D8]) at Müürivahe 12. Just outside the Old Town, behind the railway station at Kotzebue 16, is the **Dolls' Museum** (see page 127).

FURTHER WALKS

FROM THE RADISSON HOTEL Tourists staying at the Radisson Hotel [1 A3] tend to

TALLINN IN 1938

Ronald Seth, extract from 'Baltic Corner'

In the middle of Tallinn is a large asphalted space called Freedom Square. If an ugly white Lutheran church standing to one side of it were removed, it would be a much finer square than it is already. On two sides it is open, on the other two are modern buildings in the latest, yet simple, modern style. If you stand in the middle of the square – not to be recommended now that they have taken the flowerbed away – facing the double avenue of trees leading up to another church with twin spires, you will have on your left an immense building in reddy-brown glazed brick, the property of an insurance company. If you look at it close to, I think you will agree with me that it is a very ugly building. Its height and the luxury of its interior appointments, however, are impressive, and on its ground floor was the 'Corso', one of the favourite coffee-house rendezvous, where as much business was done as in a great many offices; perhaps more. The 'Corso' unfortunately is no more, and its clientele has transferred to other newer coffee-houses.

If you face this building, the EKA, on its left you will see the 'Gloria Palace', erected by

walk directly through the Viru Gate into the Old Town but if they briefly turn in the other direction they will be well rewarded. The archaeological remains of **St John's Almshouse** (see page 145 [1 A3]) on Tartu mnt are now open to the public, and the pavement has been broadened to allow access to them. Some wooden buildings a Jew, and though of simple exterior appearance it is typically flamboyant, all gilt and glittering glass inside. In the basement is a bar and restaurant with one of the best dance floors in Tallinn. To the left of the 'Gloria' is the new Palace Hotel, not quite as high as the EKA, but high enough to be impressive and again built in good simple taste.

Now turn about, and the buildings you see on this side are no less impressive. On the right are the National Art Galleries which we used to admire until the huge Eeks Maja building beside it was finished, which now makes it look rather miniature. This new house, built by the Houseowners Bank, is as high as EKA but much more attractive and, for me, more impressive, with floor upon floor of really exclusive flats and offices and modern shops beneath. Freedom Square is representative of modern Estonian architectural aspirations. Here, right in the middle of a city where ancient and modern buildings have sprung side by side with a deliberate inconsiderateness, it seems to me that in no way are these buildings covering up or spoiling the old medieval treasures.

remain on **Maakri** [1 A3] as an incongruous contrast to the increasing number of skyscrapers that surround them. Note in particular number 23, built in 1910 as a textile workshop and restored in 1996. The road sign at the corner of Maakri and Tornimäe was for many years probably unique in central Tallinn, being in Russian and

Estonian but it was finally changed into an Estonian-only one in 2005. One of the first acts of the government after the restoration of independence in 1991 was to remove Russian completely from all public places and most such street signs had been replaced, or at least had the Russian whitewashed over, by the end of 1992. The **Armenian Church** at Tartu 16a [1 A3] also looks increasingly out of place in this ultra-mercenary environment. The building was for most of its life a Catholic church but the local Armenian community took it over in 1994. Note the lack of icons inside, which distinguishes their religious practices so clearly from those of the Russian Orthodox community.

20TH-CENTURY TALLINN A walk from the Viru Gate [2 D4] along either Pärnu mnt or Estonia pst, and then along Kaarli pst back to the **National Library** [3 C8], passes the main buildings that remain from the end of the Tsarist period and the first independence period, ie: from 1900 until 1940. Jugendstil, neo-classicism and functionalism are all represented here and it is to be hoped that developers do not get permission to make drastic changes. At present the only likely change is thought to be at the Sakala Conference Centre, in fact a Soviet building, which if rebuilt could compete with the more modern facilities in the larger hotels.

The **Estonian National Theatre** [3 A5] was designed by a Finnish architect, Armas Lindgren, and opened in 1913, although the rebuilding that followed the bombing of Tallinn in 1944 was carried out under the Estonian architect Alar Kotli. The money for the original building was raised by private subscription and the Tsarist authorities attempted to block the project. They did briefly succeed in preventing the Estonian language from being used in any production. In 1918, the Estonian National Assembly met here.

On the opposite side of Estonia pst from the theatre is the **Estonian Bank Museum** (see page 132 [3 E6]), which was modernised in the summer of 1998. The **Sakala Conference Centre** [3 E6], a Soviet-era building behind the Bank Museum, is best known for the stained glass of Rait Prääts whose work can also be seen in St Nicholas's Church and in the National Library. It is thought that this area is likely to be developed soon with many office and hotel projects now under consideration.

On **Vabaduse Väljak** (Freedom Square) [3 D6], the Palace Hotel and the Town Hall beside it both date from the 1930s. Their size and the imposing nature of similar buildings along Pärnu mnt testify to the confidence of the regime at the time. Behind them are a number of functionalist buildings that survived the 1944 bombing raid. A statue of Peter the Great was erected in the square in 1910 to commemorate the 200th anniversary of the surrender of Tallinn by the Swedes to the Russians. It was removed only in 1923, several years after independence. Pictures of parades there before 1923 show Peter the Great looking down on the Estonian president. Nobody knows what happened to the top of the statue, but the metal from the base was used to mint Estonian coins. The Soviets had their parades here (when it was called Victory Square) and now each 24 February, which is National Day, there is a march past in front of the president and the prime minister. It is sad that much of this square, so important in Estonian history, is now a car park. At least the layout improved somewhat in December 2003 when the **Freedom Clock** was unveiled. This consists in fact of two towers, one in limestone with a traditional clock and one in steel with two digital timers marking the time from the first declaration of independence in February 1918 and then from the end of Soviet power in August 1991.

CHANGING TALLINN A walk again from Viru Gate across Viru Square [2 E3] gives an appropriately unflattering picture of the construction that took place between 1960 and 1980 but a more positive one of what happened between 2002 and 2004. Looking back towards Narva mnt, the **Viru Hotel** [2 E3] is a major eyesore and the inevitable result of conflicting Soviet policies in the early 1970s. On the one hand, tourists needed to be admitted to Tallinn to boost the country's international image; on the other, they needn't be allowed serious contact with the local population. An isolated tower block was obviously the answer and until 1980, when some of the Olympic Games were held in Tallinn, the Viru was the only hotel for foreigners. Many probably saw Tallinn only from the bar on the 22nd floor. Estonians console themselves with the knowledge that the Viru Hotel did at least spare them a 'Stalinist cathedral' which was one proposal for this location; an enormous memorial to Mikhail Kalinin was another idea. Kalinin, a member of Lenin's Politburo, lived in Tallinn for three years between 1901 and 1904 whilst he was banished from St Petersburg. A Soviet guidebook published in 1987 blames the lack of 'artistic and economic means' for the failure of both projects. One published a year or two later might have given the true reason: the intense local opposition. A more modest statue of Kalinin was instead erected on Tower Square, a park between the Old Town and the railway station. (As with most other Soviet statues, it was removed in the early 1990s.)

Behind the Viru Hotel is the **Kaubamaja** department store [2 E3], built in the 1960s but modernised on many occasions since. In 2004, a glass walkway linked it to the Viru Centre shopping complex built beside the hotel. In the Soviet period it was crudely divided between a shop for the local population and one for foreigners. Both were flagships in their different ways. The local shop was better supplied than most in St Petersburg and Moscow and the notorious 'Berioshka', which took only precious *valuta* (hard foreign currencies) in exchange for vodka, wooden dolls and fur hats, was the only Soviet shop that thousands of tourists would ever enter. In the 1990s Viru Square was a dismal muddle of kiosks, bus stops and car parks. In 2002 and 2003 it was a building site but by April 2004 it had been completely transformed into a modern shopping centre with an extended Viru Hotel on one side and the Tallink Hotel on the other.

Before the war, the main Tallinn synagogue existed on this site where Kaubamaja now stands. The current **synagogue** [1 B2] shares premises with the Jewish School on Karu, near the harbour, and was opened in December 2000. It is the only active synagogue in Estonia and replaced a temporary building used in Soviet times on Magdaleena Street in the southern part of the city. Sadly, the occasional brutal attack on the premises has meant that they carry no outside identification. The building is now the headquarters for the small Jewish community in Tallinn. Visitors, both Jewish and non-Jewish, are welcome to visit the synagogue. A new building for the synagogue alone began in late 2005 next to the current site.

Returning towards town, Karu becomes Ahtri which skirts the harbour. This will soon be an area of considerable development. Having been a totally closed area in Soviet times, it was suddenly abandoned in 1991 when Soviet troops pulled out and most of the buildings were left to decay. It is likely to become an extension of the financial quarter now rising along Narva mnt.

10 What to See and Do

If you have only one day in Tallinn, make sure you visit the superb KUMU Art Museum (see page 129) and the City Museum (see page 126). Of the churches, don't miss the Dome Church (page 151) for its impressive tombs.

MUSEUMS

Most museums close at least one day a week – usually Monday or Tuesday – and some for two days; they also close on public holidays. Many do not open until 11.00; Kadriorg Palace, KUMU and the Mikkel Museum stay open until 21.00 on Thursdays in summer. Churches are open every day from around 09.00.

The most popular ones for foreign visitors, such as Kadriorg Palace and those listed above, charge around 50EEK for adults. Others charge around 25EEK. Most give reductions for children and for senior citizens. Many of the museums don't charge on 21 February (International Guides Day) and 18 May (International Museums Day). There is also often one day a month when free admission is granted, although the day in question varies. Several state museums share the website www.ekm.ee, and several city ones www.linnamuuseum.ee. These and the individual sites listed below give current information on opening hours and on charges. The Tallinn Card gives free admission to all the museums listed.

ADAMSON-ERIC MUSEUM *Lühike Jalg 3;* ℡ *644 5838; www.ekm.ee; open Wed–Sun 11.00–18.00* [3 C5]

Adamson-Eric (1902–68) was without doubt the most famous Estonian artist who worked during both the independence period and the Soviet era. This house has no links with him, although before being used as a museum it did have workshops for coppersmiths. The museum opened in 1983 and the collection is based on around 1,000 works bequeathed by his widow. These cover his whole life in both painting and applied art. Gifts from abroad have recently been added to the collection. Labels are in English. Adamson-Eric's parents were able to pay for long periods of study during the 1920s in both Paris and Berlin. Elements of Fauvism and Cubism can be seen in many of his pictures but he was equally drawn to the Bauhaus and worked closely with Walter Gropius, George Grosz and Otto Dix. On his return to Estonia he first specialised in portraits, then added landscapes and broadened into applied arts. In this field, his work became as diverse as his painting. Around 1930, he began with tapestries and textiles and then added ceramics and metalwork to his range. Shortly before the war he diversified even more, starting to work with leather and to design stage sets. He retreated with the Soviet army in 1941 and managed to maintain his artistic integrity despite the stringent demands of Soviet officialdom. With the inevitable lack of materials for applied art at this time, he concentrated again on painting. In 1949, the political tide finally turned against him and he was expelled from the Communist Party, forced to give up his posts and sent into factory work. Although released in 1953 on Stalin's death, his health had deteriorated and he suffered a stroke in 1955. His reaction was simply to learn to paint as well with his left hand as he had previously done with his right! His health slowly improved and he was able to add porcelain painting and tile design to his work in the field of applied art. He remained active until shortly before his death in 1968.

APPLIED ARTS MUSEUM *Lai 17;* ✎ *641 1927; www.ekm.ee; open Wed–Sun 11.00–18.00* [2 B3]
The ticket desk still sells the Soviet guidebook which boasts that the exhibits 'are really wonderful, conspicuous in their originality and can bear comparison with the best items of the world'. Exhibits from the Soviet period are now on the upper floors, and modern ones on the ground floor, so visitors can judge the changes for themselves and whether such hyperbole applies to either era. In all fields the collections are extensive and show the Estonian dedication to pottery, weaving, glassmaking and woodwork that has surmounted all political regimes.

ARCHITECTURE MUSEUM *Ahtri 2;* ✎ *625 7000; www. arhitektuurimuuseum.ee; open Wed–Sun 11.00–18.00 Oct 1–May 18, and in summer Wed–Fri 12.00– 20.00, Sat–Sun 11.00–18.00; admission 30EEK* [1 A2]
As a limestone building dating from 1908, this is one of the very few left from the time

when the whole area around the harbour was industrial. Still often called Rotermann Salt Storage after its first owner and its first role, it now stands out against a background of office development and some plots of land still abandoned. As a sensitive security zone in Soviet times, little rebuilding took place in this area then, but the pace of activity since 1991 has certainly made up for it. Evening opening in the summer often enables tourists to add a visit here to one of the Old Town in the afternoon.

The building was renovated in 1995 with the aim of housing such a museum. The basement houses the permanent exhibition, which covers all the styles of architecture prevalent in Estonia during the 20th century and also shows plans of some of the buildings from which Tallinn was fortunately spared. The display concentrates on the work of local architects and so the materials they preferred: limestone, dolomite and oak. Higher floors have changing exhibitions, but again these are always on an architectural theme. The bookshop here is the best source of English-language material on architecture and a considerable quantity has recently been published in Estonia.

CITY MUSEUM *Vene 17;* ↘ *644 6553; www.linnamuuseum.ee; open Mon, Wed–Mon 10.30–18.00* [2 C3]
Many of the exhibits here would now be regarded as politically incorrect in the West as they concentrate on the accoutrements of the rich; life below stairs and outside the guilds and churches is ignored. Part of the museum is quite understandably called the 'Treasury', given the quantity of tapestries, silverware, pewter and porcelain displayed there. Nonetheless, the collection shows the

breadth of industry and culture that developed in Tallinn from 1860 onwards. The arrival in 1870 of the railway from St Petersburg led to an increase in the population from 30,000 to 160,000 by 1917. One anniversary the Estonians were forced to celebrate in 1910 was the 200th anniversary of the Russian conquest. The museum was closed in 2000 for extensive renovations which included proper lighting and the addition of considerable visual material. It now shows videos of pre-war and Soviet Estonia, of the 1944 bombing, the 1980 Olympics and the 1989 demonstrations that would in due course lead to independence. Allow at least an hour to see these properly. A room of Soviet and Nazi posters has also been added. The café on the top floor is unusual in offering only homemade food. This museum is well labelled in English and the postcard sets they sell are excellent value.

DOLLS' MUSEUM *Kotzebue 16;* ☏ *641 3491; www.linnamuuseum.ee; open Wed–Sun 10.30–18.00*
Opened in 1985 as a memorial to one of Lenin's closest colleagues, Mikhail Kalinin, the Dolls' Museum nonetheless even then had a small collection of toys. Kalinin is now forgotten and toys have taken over completely. The collection of dolls and dolls' houses goes back as far as the 18th century, but there are also board games, teddy bears and general toys from 1900 onwards since this is one of the few elements of Estonian life unaffected by the changing political environment. The walk from the Old Town behind the Hotel Skane offers a completely changed architectural environment; Tallinn on the wrong side of the tracks becomes a town of poorly

maintained wooden houses and an abandoned factory. The market beside the station is worth a stop of a few minutes. Excellent light refreshments are available at prices well below those elsewhere in the town and the choice of clothes, CDs and gadgets is a good reflection of mass Estonian and local Russian taste.

EDUARD VILDE MUSEUM *Roheline 3;* ☏ *601 3181; www.linnamuuseum.ee/vilde; open Wed–Mon 11.00–18.00* [1 C3]
On leaving the Mikkel Museum (see page 000 for details) and turning left, you will come to this splendidly isolated house at Roheline 3 where Estonia's most prolific writer, both at home and in exile all over Europe, spent the final six years of his life between 1927 and 1933. Typically for most established Estonians at that time, the furnishings are simple and there are many empty spaces.

ENERGY MUSEUM *Põhja pst 29;* ☏ *612 4500; www.energiakeskus.ee; open Mon–Sat 10.00–17.00*
For many years after independence was restored, this museum remained ultra-Soviet with graphs displaying uninterrupted progress in all technological fields from 1945 until the late 1980s. It has now largely changed into a teenagers' theme park, with plenty of possibilities for hands-on displays on all forms of energy, including how they are generated and distributed. Although little is written in English here (and the website is totally in Estonian) these young visitors are happy to try out their English on foreigners wanting to join in the fun.

ESTONIAN ART MUSEUM (KUMU EESTI KUNSTIMUUSEUM) *Weizenbergi 34/Valge 1;*
☎ 644 9139; www.kumu.ee; open May–Sep, Tue–Sun 11.00–18.00; Oct–Apr,
Wed–Sun 11.00–18.00. Late–night opening on Thu until 21.00) [1 D3]

It is not surprising that the Queen's visit to Tallinn in October 2006 centred on
KUMU; finally the capital city can boast of a museum devoted almost entirely to work
by Estonians. KUMU is an abbreviation of the Estonian word *Kunstimuuseum* – Art
Museum, but it is in fact much more than that. 'Arts Centre' would probably be the
best description as KUMU is just as eager to encourage new art as it is to promote
its long-standing collection. About half its space will be devoted to exhibitions rather
than to permanent displays.

This is also one of the very few buildings in the Baltics constructed specifically for
a collection. Normally it has been the other way around, with collections having to fit
into a building that happens to be available. This was in fact the fate of this collection
for many years, when it was housed in the Estonian Knighthood building opposite the
Dome Church at the top of Toompea. However, when in 1993 a competition was
announced for a new art gallery to be housed in Kadriorg Park, Estonians knew that
in due course their art would be displayed in suitable surroundings, with appropriate
space and light. The winner of the competition was the Finnish architect Pekka
Vapaavuori. Construction only started in 2002 and KUMU finally opened in February
2006.

A few of the paintings on display have been in state hands since 1920, but many
had to be hidden during the war and under the Soviet occupation. Although, much of

what might have been here was destroyed during World War II or shortly afterwards, much was preserved, often at great risk to the artists and their collectors.

Those with a political interest in Estonia will probably want to visit the fourth floor first, where art produced during the Soviet era is displayed. Artists working at that time had the same dilemmas as their colleagues in the music and literary fields. It was possible to acquiesce totally to the demands of Moscow or, with subtle scheming, to maintain some artistic and Estonian integrity. Hence the name of this gallery is 'Difficult Choices'. The demands of Moscow did, of course, change considerably between 1945 and 1990, and the work shown here reflects this. The abstract sculpture Pegasus by **Edgar Viies** (b1931) produced in 1963 could not have been displayed publicly much earlier and might well have faced disapproval again during the stagnant period of the early 1980s. (It was originally produced for the restaurant on Harju which still carries this name.) From a distance, the industrial landscapes of **Lepo Mikko** (1911–78) might seem to be purely political, but closer inspection will reveal a wide range of human expressions and varied use of colour. Some of the art shown from the 1950s, like the blocks of flats in the vicinity of KUMU, could have been produced anywhere from East Berlin to Vladivostok. There were understandable objections to showing such work here, but future generations of Estonians need to be aware of what happened in their country during the 1950s, the toughest decade of the Soviet era.

Earlier Estonian art is shown on the third floor, most of it dating from the late 19th century until 1940. **Gregor von Bochmann** (1850–1930) is often regarded as the first real Estonian artist even though he spent most of his life in Germany. He did however paint Estonian peasants and their meagre surroundings, which differentiates him from earlier Baltic Germans who only painted each other or idealised rural scenes. **Konrad Mägi** (1878–1925) is probably the artist best known outside Estonia and perhaps that is why his paintings still command higher prices than those of any other Estonian painter. He was one of the founders of the Pallas School of Art in Tartu (a hotel with this name now stands on the site) which encouraged diversity and travel amongst its pupils, and so was immediately closed down by the Soviet authorities in 1940. Impressionism had a great influence on his work. France was also to influence one of his best students, **Karl Pärsimägi** (1902–42), whose political involvement there was to lead to his death in Auschwitz after he was caught trying to help French Jews.

The second floor is reserved for temporary exhibitions, which in the summer will always have an Estonian theme. In the auditorium on the first floor (ground floor for British readers) KUMU aims to branch out into other cultural fields, so it will hold film shows, concerts and performances. The second floor also has a restaurant which overlooks Kadriorg Park and which is open in the evenings. The museum is fully accessible to the disabled.

KUMU sadly adopts the restricted opening hours of so many Estonian museums and in closing on several Estonian holidays during the summer (23/24 Jun, 20 Aug) which happen to coincide with the peak tourist season. In good weather, a pleasant way to reach KUMU is to take tram No 1 or 3 from the Viru Hotel to the final stop at Kadriorg. It is then about a ten-minute walk through the park, past the Palace and the President's House. Otherwise buses 31, 67 and 68 from Kunstiakadeemia on Gonsiori near the Viru Hotel stop behind KUMU.

ESTONIAN BANK MUSEUM *Estonia pst 11; ☎ 668 0760; www.eestipank.info; open Wed–Fri 12.00–17.00, Sat 11.00–16.00; admission free* [3 E6]
The political history of the country is mirrored in this museum through its currency. In 1928, the kroon was tied to the British pound but it floated after 1933 when Britain left the Gold Standard. The current building dates from 1935 and manages to combine elements of neo-Gothic, neo-Renaissance and functionalism. In its predecessor, Estonian independence was proclaimed on 24 February 1918 and in this one a temporary Estonian government was formed in September 1944 between the German and the Russian occupations. The collections here are always bang up to date, so include not only the banknotes issued since 1992, but also designs for recent credit cards and even those for Estonian euro coins unlikely to be introduced until 2008.

ESTONIAN HISTORY MUSEUM *Pikk 17; ☎ 641 1630; www.earn.ee; open Thu–Tue 11.00–18.00* [2 C4]
Dating from 1410, it was the headquarters of the Great Guild and has changed little since. Visitors who arrive when the museum is shut can at least be consoled by the sight of the 15th-century door knockers. Exhibits inside are well labelled in English

and concentrate on archaeology and costumes. Of more contemporary interest is the coin collection and a section on the founding of the local freemasons in the late 1770s. They were later banned by Alexander I in 1822. It has to be admitted however, that Estonian history is better covered in Tartu than in Tallinn. Do not miss the 20-minute film shown regularly here in the alcove off the main hall as it illustrates the archaeological links Estonia has with its neighbouring countries and then the influence of the Hanseatic League on so many of its early buildings.

FIRE-FIGHTING MUSEUM *Vana-Viru 14;* ↘ *644 4251; www.rescue.ee; open Tue–Sat 12.00–17.00* [2 E3]
The museum on this site was due to close in autumn 2006 but it is likely to reopen in premises on Rau mnt, parallel to Narva mnt, some time in 2007. Like the Energy Museum, it has not changed since the Soviet era so combines the didactic with the heroic. Dolls' houses show every possible cause of an accident in each room. Macabre photos abound of charred bodies, exploding television sets and open fires out of control. A panel lists medals awarded to local firemen until 1988 but none is listed after that year. It is a cruel comment to suggest that heroism in the Estonian fire service ceased at the restoration of independence in 1991. A number of horse-drawn and early motor fire engines are displayed. There are dramatic pictures of the 1920 St Olav's fire and photographs taken illegally in 1982 of the collapsed spire at St Nicholas. Although captions to all exhibits are only in Estonian and Russian, the staff hand out translation cards in English and German.

HEALTH MUSEUM *Lai 28-30; ℄ 641 1732; www.tervishoiumuuseum.ee; open Tue–Sat 11.00–18.00* [2 B3]

The building here dates from 1377 and a spiral stone staircase remains from that time. The Health Museum is one of the few totally contemporary museums in Tallinn and uses a range of models, toys, visual aids and colourful charts to show both adults and children the importance of healthy living. One cabinet shows the ideal weekly diet for a ten-year-old child. Some visitors may find the explicit illustrations of the effects of syphilis disturbing. Similarly blunt are the mummified remains of an alcoholic chain-smoking 54 year old compared with the healthy organs of a car-crash victim. If these are not warning enough, the lungs of active and passive smokers are shown, together with a cirrhosis-ridden liver.

Overall, it is a brightly lit and well-thought-out display, a vivid contrast to many other museums. It may well be the only museum in the country with a hands-on element – two exercise bicycles are available for visitors. One section has been translated into Russian – that on sexually transmitted diseases. More conventional museum exhibits include medical equipment from 100 years or so ago.

KADRIORG PALACE *Weizenbergi 37; ℄ 606 6400; www.ekm.ee; open Tue–Sun 10.00–17.00, open Thu in summer 10.00–21,00* [1 D2]

The centrepiece of Kadriorg Park is the palace. It was built immediately following Peter the Great's first visit to Tallinn in 1718 with his Italian architect Niccolo Michetti. The triumphal decoration of the ceiling in the Great Hall celebrates his defeat of the Swedes in the Northern War and is loosely based on Rembrandt's *Diana and Actaeon*. The hunter being torn apart by his dogs can be seen to symbolise the Swedish King Charles XII being let down by his army. Sadly the building was not completed by 1725 when Peter the Great died and no subsequent tsar ever showed the commitment that he did. In fact Catherine I never came to Tallinn again after his death. Perhaps the description often given of the palace as a 'mini-Versailles' is fair, as what was carried out does show some French and Italian influence. A fire destroyed much of the interior in 1750 and it was subsequently never again used by the Russian royal family. In 1930, Kadriorg Palace became the official residence of the Estonian president but now houses the **Foreign Art Museum**, the collection being mainly Flemish and Baltic German.

None of the furniture was originally here. The Russian royal family took furniture with them as they travelled between their palaces and also 'borrowed' extensively from the local nobility. Much of this collection is what the Baltic Germans had to leave in their manor houses when Hitler 'called them home' in October 1939. Despite the cool personal and state relations with the Russians, a lot of furniture was still ordered from St Petersburg during the first independence period (1920–40). However, the room devoted to Soviet art from the 1920s is likely to be of most interest to visitors. The designs on the porcelain show the most immediate break with the past as all the themes are 100% political. It would take another ten years before painting was similarly controlled. Some of this porcelain was prepared for the first Soviet Art Exhibition held in St Petersburg in 1923, by which time the St Petersburg Imperial Porcelain Factory had become the State Porcelain Factory. It came to be known as 'agitprop'. Many rooms have been restored to their original 1930s' layout, when President Päts lived here. The Danzig-Baroque library is the most elaborate room and was completed only in 1939, a year before the Soviet takeover. The salon has a wooden drinks cabinet with panels portraying scenes from *Kalevipoeg*, the 19th-century Estonian national epic. The palace reopened in 2000 and then work started on re-landscaping the surrounding gardens. Much of this exterior work was completed in 2005.

A cottage in the park used by Peter the Great during the construction of the palace now poses as a museum [1 D3] but the paucity of exhibits perhaps redefines the word 'minimalist'. A bare main room, and some haphazard items of furniture would be best concealed from tourists entitled to expect much more. The only redeeming feature is the attic, which displays a series of photographs of Tallinn from the late 19th and early 20th centuries. The toilets are very cramped, so presumably they do not date from Peter's time, given that he was 2m tall.

KALEV CHOCOLATE MUSEUM *Pikk 16;* ☎ *628 3811; www.kalev.ee; open Mon–Sat 09.30–18.00; admission free* [2 C3]

Now based at Pikk 16, above Maiasmokk Café, the Kalev Chocolate Museum originally opened in December 2000 beside the Kalev factory on the Pärnu road to the south of Tallinn, near the tram terminus. In 2003, the factory moved out of Tallinn and that part of the building was taken over by the police, although the amount of computer theft that accompanied this move caused them considerable embarrassment and the local population considerable amusement. Whilst the museum gives a thorough coverage of the different production techniques used in its 200-year history and visitors have the chance to smell eight different flavours, the real interest is in the political history revealed in the designs on the boxes issued during the Soviet period. In 1950, the tenth anniversary of Estonia 'joining' the USSR warranted a special box-top, even though three of those years had been spent under German occupation. Later in the 1950s, pre-war pictures of Narva were used, even though it was the Soviet army that destroyed the city in 1944. By the 1980s the authorities became aware of the knowledge Estonians now had of the West, so Mickey Mouse and Finnish television characters were allowed to join traditional Russian role models.

The history of chewing-gum in the former USSR deserves a book to itself since different politburos all devoted endless sessions to this topic. Puritans wanted it banned but the realists wanted to prove that whatever the US could do, the USSR could do better. Production was first authorised in 1968, banned again and then reintroduced for the Olympics. Only the Kalev factory ever received the necessary authorisation.

The factory is proud that following independence in 1991 it has been able to re-establish export markets, even as far away as the United States. Perhaps a few elderly consumers there remember the Shirley Temple portrait used on boxes produced in the 1930s. Not even famous German factories are likely to be able to match the 237 varieties of marzipan produced by Kalev now. Prices in this new museum are a little higher than in most local shops, but of course the choice available is greater. In 2006, some of the upstairs rooms belonging to the museum were still closed.

KIEK IN DE KÖK *Komandandi 2;* ✆ *644 6686; www.linnamuuseum.ee/kiekindekok; open Tue–Sun 10.30–18.00* [3 C6]

The construction of Tallinn's city wall began in 1265 and took 300 years to complete. Once finished, it was over 2km long, often 3m thick, and with 35 watch towers; 26 of these towers survive, as does about two-thirds of the wall. From its initial construction in the 15th century until its completion in the late 17th century, this tower grew in height and width, with walls and floors as thick as 4m, but ironically, after a Russian attack in 1577, it never saw military action again. In 1709, Tallinn's fate for the next two centuries was sealed at the Battle of Poltsava, when Peter the Great defeated Charles XII, but this was hundreds of kilometres away, in what is now Ukraine. The last time the tower was prepared for war was in the 1850s when the Russians feared a British invasion during the Crimean War. On the top floor, note the model of the 'plague doctor' with a waxed tunic and cape impregnated with herbs. He carries a cane with which to touch patients to avoid any risk of infection. The main exhibition on the top three floors covers Tallinn's military history. The lower floors are now used as an art gallery. In 2008 the tunnels under the city wall should be open and one of the entrances will be here.

Kiek in de Kök

KUMU see *Estonian Art Museum*, page 129.

MARITIME MUSEUM (*Pikk 70;* ✆ *641 1408; www.tallinn.ee/meremuuseum; open Wed–Sun 10.00–18.00*) [2 C1]

Fat Margaret, the tower which holds this museum, was built between 1510 and 1529. Some walls are as much as 6m thick. In 1830, it became a prison but after being stormed in 1917 it was left as a ruin for the next 60 years. Polish restorers, famous throughout the former Soviet block, finally came to the rescue in 1978. Climb to the roof for very photogenic views of St Olav's and the town gates. The museum covers shipbuilding, cartography, port construction and fish breeding. There is a recent exhibit on the *Estonia* which sank off the Finnish coast on 28 September 1994 with the loss of 850 lives. A model of one of the boats has political interest. It was originally named after Viktor Kingissepp, leader of the underground Estonian Communist Party in the early 1920s who was executed in 1922 after leading a failed attempt to overthrow the government. In 1990, it was renamed after Gustav Sule, who was Estonian javelin champion in the 1930s.

MIKKEL MUSEUM *Weizenberg 28;* ✆ *601 5844; www.etm.ee; open Tue–Sun 10.00–17.00, Thu in summer 10.00–21.00* [1 D3]

Opposite the main entrance to Kadriorg Palace is the Mikkel Museum. The building was the palace kitchen but in 1997 was opened to house the collection of Estonia's most fortunate private art collector, Johannes Mikkel. Born in 1907, he was able to start buying during the first independence period when departing Baltic Germans and Russian nobles abandoned enormous quantities of paintings, porcelain and prints. He was allowed to trade during the Soviet period and enhanced his collection with items bought in the Caucasus and central Asia. There is no predominant theme, but the quality and taste of every item stands out, be it a piece of Kangxi or Meissen porcelain, a Dürer woodcut, a Rembrandt etching or any one of his 20 Flemish paintings. Folders in English are available in every room with descriptions of all major exhibits and modern lighting ensures that each item is viewed as well as possible. Mikkel died in January 2006 so perhaps the museum will soon be enhanced with further pieces from his private collection and a memoir to explain how he could enjoy such a capitalist lifestyle for so long.

NATIONAL LIBRARY *Tõnismägi 2; ☏ 630 7611; www.nlib.ee; open Mon–Fri 10.00–20.00, Sat 12.00–19.00, closed Sat in Jul and Aug* [3 C8]
Day tickets for the National Library may be bought in the entrance hall, a section of which is decorated with prints by one of Estonia's most famous 20th-century artists, Eduard Wiiralt. Sadly these are not lit as well as they should be. To encourage regular use, the library has several music rooms, antiquarian and modern bookshops, a café and even piped music. On a bitter winter's day tourists may wish to await a change in the weather amongst the many English-language books and journals now available there. As one of Estonia's many preparations for entry into the EU, there are also large French, German and Scandinavian reading rooms. Normally, however, visitors should head straight for the eighth floor to view two contrasting Tallinns. To the north and east is the Tallinn of the travel posters – the spires, turrets and golden

domes. In the other direction is a part of the town best seen at this distance, consisting of abandoned factories and fading tower blocks, with minimal intrusion of any colour. This area is still changing too slowly.

The predecessor to this library was opened in 1918 in the parliament building on Toompea and had 2,000 books, a number that only increased to 6,000 during the 1930s. After World War II, the history of the library mirrored that of the country as a whole. Its bleakest period was until 1953 when most of the collection was of Russian books translated into Estonian. On Stalin's death the library was renamed after one of Estonia's most famous authors, Friedrich Reinhold Kreutzwald, a clear sign of a more liberal climate. By 1967, funds were specifically allocated for books in the Estonian language and in 1988, shortly before this new building was supposed to open, it was renamed the National Library and the formerly restricted sections were opened to all. The design seems to symbolise glasnost: light streams in through many massive windows and large open shelves display a wide cross-section of the two million books stored there. It will remain a grandiose memorial to massive public- sector investment. Yet it was almost not completed. The fading Soviet government was not eager to continue funding projects outside Russia and the new Estonian one was faced with bills it could not pay. On 28 June 1989, between four and five thousand volunteers joined the building works under the slogan 'Dig a grave for Stalinism'. The director, Ivi Eenmaa, later to become mayor of Tallinn, single-handedly fought Moscow and then each new Estonian government for adequate funds and was finally able to open the library on 22 February 1993, two days before National Day. Many Estonians would have liked to remove the Soviet War Memorial from the front of the museum, particularly as the sculpture is of a Red Army soldier. In 2006 the memorial became the subject of a major dispute between the national government, which wanted to remove it to a less prominent location, and the town, which was willing to accede to the demands of the Russian-speaking population that it should stay. On 22 September, the anniversary of Tallinn's 'reoccupation' or 'liberation' in 1944, rival Estonian and Russian demonstrations took place here. A constant police guard was then mounted to prevent further access from either faction.

NATURAL HISTORY MUSEUM *Lai 29a;* ☏ *641 1738; www.loodusmuuseum.ee; open Wed–Sun 10.00–17.00* [2 B2]
The surprise here is that most of the exhibits are contemporary rather than historical. Whilst there is an impressive array of stuffed animals, of far greater interest perhaps is the collection of photographs of the Estonian countryside, all well lit and well labelled. The standard of English is particularly high here.

OCCUPATION MUSEUM *Toompea 8;* ☏ *650 5281; www.okupatsioon.ee; open Tue–Sun 11.00–18.00* [3 C7]
This museum could only be opened thanks to funds provided by an Estonian-American Olga Ritso, who fled abroad in 1944 after both her father and her uncle had been killed by the Soviets. When the museum was formally opened by her

and Prime Minister Juhan Parts, they cut not a ribbon but barbed wire. The pathetically inadequate clothing of the prison camps is perhaps the most moving exhibit though the sight of small cases into which thousands of Estonians had to pack belongings for their Siberian exile must run a close second. The red star and a swastika are always shown side by side. To the Estonians, the Russians and the Germans are equally guilty. There are also display cases showing day-to-day life in Estonia under Soviet rule. It seems hard to believe that these items were all most Estonians knew until 1991. The cellars are now being used to display statues from Soviet times, which had all been pulled down when Estonian independence was restored in 1991. One earlier one is however missing. A statue of Stalin which had survived since 1956 could not be included; being 4m high there was no way it could be brought into the museum for display. The entrance to the museum is on Toompea, not on Pärnu.

PARK MUSEUM *Weizenbergi 26; tel: 601 4548; www.ekm.ee; open Tue–Sun 10.00–17.00; Thu in summer 10.00–21.00* [1 C3]
In the summer of 2006 the Kadriorg Park Museum was opened next to the Mikkel Museum, perhaps a little before it was really ready. For now, it is more interesting as a turn-of-the-century private house, but as its collection increases, it should show how the design of the park has changed under different governments. Displays are planned of archaeological finds that include weapons discovered in the area dating from 13th-century battles for Tallinn.

PARLIAMENT *Lossi plats 1a;* ☎ *631 6331; www.riigikogu.ee; open when Parliament is in session* [3 B6]

The façade is a simple classicist one, and all the stone and wooden materials are local. Earlier buildings on this site had usually served as a governor's residence although, in the late 19th century, the building became a prison. The earliest fort was built on this site in 1227 and the northern and western walls date from this time.

The most famous room within the building is the White Hall, with its balcony overlooking the square. The current décor, with white cornices and a yellow ceiling, dates from 1935. From 1922 there had been a more elaborate neo-classicist design, including ceiling mirrors and elaborate panelling. The current Parliamentary Chamber was rebuilt in 1998 and members of the public can attend debates there, but no interpretation from Estonian is provided. There are 101 Members of Parliament, representing ten parties and around 20% of its members are women. Visitors are forbidden to enter 'with cold steel, firearms and pungent-smelling substances'.

PHARMACY *Raekoja plats 11;* ☎ *631 4860; open daily 10.00–18.00* [2 C4]

Tour guides often like to point out that this business opened 70 years before Columbus discovered America. The coat of arms of the Burchart family, who ran the pharmacy for 400 years, can be seen over the entrance. Amongst the medicines they dispensed which are unlikely to find contemporary favour were fishes' eyes, lambswool and ground rubies, but patients were at least offered these potions with a glass of hot wine to help digestion. In 1725, Peter the Great summoned Burchart to

St Petersburg, but he died before Burchart could reach him. In 2000, the pharmacy was extensively refurbished. Part of it is a museum and part a modern chemist's shop.

PHOTOGRAPHIC MUSEUM *Raekoja tn 4–6;* \ *644 8767; www.linnamuuseum.ee; open Thu–Tue 10.30–18.00* [2 C4]
Estonia has always had a strong photographic tradition and this museum displays not only cameras produced in the country but also photographs from the 19th and early 20th centuries. The earliest date from 1840. We tend to think of business cards with photos as fairly new but the museum displays one printed in 1859. April fools with cameras started a little later, in the 1890s, so canals in Pisa and leaning towers in Venice date from then. The Minox camera was produced commercially in Riga from 1938, but the first ones to be made came from Tallinn in 1936, with several prototypes being displayed here. It is fortunate that many pictures from the first independence period have survived. Each year one aspect of the collection is enlarged for a temporary exhibition. In 2005 it was centred on postcards and in 2006 on church interiors, which showed how active churches have been recently with restoration work. One British custom has been taken over by Estonian photographers: everybody says 'cheese' in English and it is also the name of the local photographic journal. The basement is a gallery for the display and sale of contemporary photographs.

ST JOHN'S ALMSHOUSE *Tartu Road;* \ *644 6553; www.linnamuuseum.ee/jaaniseek; open Wed–Sun 10.30–18.00* [1 A3]

This museum is built over part of the pavement near the junction of Tartu mnt and Ravala pst. The foundations of the building date from the early 13th century, as does the neighbouring cemetery, but neither were discovered until 2001 during a road-widening project on Tartu mnt. Luckily it was possible to implement this scheme and grant access to the foundations, which are now protected and covered. The museum exhibits a wide range of finds from the site, including several skeletons. The original building was destroyed in the Livonian War towards the end of the 16th century but those that followed were all used as hospitals or centres for the elderly. The last one was pulled down in the 1960s.

There is a separate, constantly running film show about Kivisilla, which was regarded as a suburb of Tallinn until as late as the 19th century. With its many small factories and workshops, it could not be more different from the skyscrapers for offices and hotels that arise all around today.

TAMMSAARE MUSEUM *Koidula 12a;* ✎ *601 3232; www.linnamuuseum.ee/tammsaare; open Wed–Mon 10.00–17.00* [1 C3]
This museum is named after and in honour of Estonia's most famous author, A H Tammsaare. The only English translations of his works were published in Moscow in the 1970s but are now out of print. Exhibits are labelled in Estonian and Russian only.

The exhibition has hardly been changed since the Soviet era so it presents him as far more of a 'man of the people' than was really the case. Tammsaare is depicted on the

25EEK note and it is perhaps significant that it is his farm that is pictured on the reverse, not this townhouse. A complete renovation of the museum began in late 2006, hopefully this will include adding descriptions in English.

THEATRE AND MUSIC MUSEUM Müürivahe 12; ☎ 644 6407;
www.tallinn.ee/teatrijamuusikamuuseum; open Wed–Sun 10.00–17.30 [3 D5]
Despite its name, this museum in fact deals only with music. A violin-maker's workshop has been reconstructed and the display covers most instruments of the orchestra, all of which have at some time been made in Estonia. The production of violins and pianos has a long and distinguished history in Tallinn, both of models and of instruments to be played. One violin model uses a hair from a one-year-old child. New instruments continue to be added to the collection, the most modern being a harpsichord from 2002. Another recent development is the naming of the tower above the museum after the composer Arvo Pärt; its walls carry both formal and informal pictures of him. It is worth paying 25EEK extra to hear the music boxes and whichever other instruments the curators care to play. They also sell tapes, for those still able to play them.

Very few labels are in English but, fortunately, this does not matter too much given the self-explanatory nature of the exhibits. Estonians are often accused of taking themselves too seriously; from the cartoons on the stairs, it is clear that Estonian musicians, at least, do not. No famous 20th-century conductor is spared portrayal in irreverent clothes. One violinist, Hugo Schuts, is even drawn in a bathing costume.

Sometimes the cartoons are replaced by pictures of Estonia's most diverse musician, Vladimir Sapoznin (1906–96), who began his career at the age of five in a circus and retired only when he was 80. He was already sufficiently well known at the age of nine to be brought to the attention of Tsar Nicholas II, who gave him a set of tin soldiers. Whatever Estonia's political background, he whistled, he sang in five different languages, he played at least ten instruments, and he popularised step-dancing. In short, he brought constant musical happiness. Sadly, he is now largely forgotten and few recordings or films remain to show his brilliance to subsequent generations.

TOWN HALL *Raekoja plats 1; ℘ 645 7900; www.tallinn.ee/raekoda; open 15 May–15 Sep 11.00–18.00* [2 C4]

The exterior and the interior are equally impressive. It was the administrative and judicial centre of the town and the extensive range of woodwork and paintings in the Council Chamber mainly reflect judicial themes. Six centuries of Tallinn's history have been determined in this room and, with the restoration of independence, its role will now increase. For much of this time there were clearly ample funds in the public treasury, as is shown by the opulence of the candelabra, the money-chests and the size of the wine cellars. One of the carvings on the magistrates' bench, of David and Goliath, is often taken to symbolise the relationship between Tallinn Council and its nominal masters on Toompea in the Old Town. The Council Chamber has always been heated, unlike the neighbouring Citizens Hall. Dancing, eating and drinking at winter receptions tend to be particularly vigorous to compensate for this. The original weathervane on the top of the spire, known as Old Thomas, was destroyed in the 1944 raid but the rest of the building was spared. German architects, artists and craftsmen were employed for the Town Hall and all documents were written only in German, even during the long periods of Swedish and Russian rule. Only the tapestries have a non-German origin, being Flemish. The originals are not in fact displayed any more, because of their fragile condition, but two exact copies woven over a six-month period in 2003 by the British company Hines of Oxford now hang in the Citizens Chamber. Both are over 8m long and show scenes from the legend of King Solomon.

It is sometimes possible to climb up the spire; the view from the top offers excellent shots of the Old Town for photographers but the stairs are steep so this is only recommended for the fit and determined. A large exhibition opened in the basement in summer 2003 and it is worth braving the extremely narrow staircase down to it. Plans and photographs of the square are shown as it has been, as it might have been and as it may be, together with many fragments unearthed in recent excavations. Do not forget to use the toilets here as they have been skilfully placed within the foundations.

Another exhibition opened in summer 2004 in the attic behind the clock. Its main exhibit is a model of Tallinn as it was in 1825, but more important is the fact that this attic has been cleared. Restoration that started in 1952 finally came to an end 52 years later. It generated 273 tonnes of debris, much of which had been stored here. Some of the smaller, more valuable finds in wood, earthenware and textiles are now on display beside the model.

CHURCHES

ALEXANDER NEVSKY CATHEDRAL ⌕ *644 3484; open daily 08.00–19.00* [3 B6]
The cathedral was built in 1900 on a former garden which had housed a statue of Martin Luther. It was Alexander Nevsky who defeated the Teutonic Knights in 1242 so the building had a dual role in pretending to show Russian superiority over both the Baltic Germans and the local Estonians. It was hoped that it would help to stifle the burgeoning nationalistic movements in Estonia, too. Ironically, the Tsarist power that it represented was to last only a further 17 years. Entering the cathedral represents a symbolic departure from Estonia. No-one speaks Estonian and no books are sold in Estonian. The icons, the mosaics and the 15-tonne bell were all imported from St Petersburg. Occasionally plans are discussed, as they were in the 1930s, for the removal of the cathedral as it is so architecturally and politically incompatible with everything else in Toompea, but it is unlikely that any government would risk the inevitable hostility that would arise amongst the Russian-speaking population of Tallinn.

Alexander Nevsky Cathedral

150

CHARLES'S CHURCH ↘ 611 9100; www.eelk.ee/tallinna.kaarli; open daily 10.00–17.00 [3 C8]

This massive and austere late 19th-century limestone building seats 1,500 people. At a time when Russian rule was becoming more oppressive, its size discreetly symbolised Estonian nationalism. It was therefore appropriate that Lennart Meri's funeral service in March 2006 was held at this church, and thousands paid their last respects as his coffin lay in state here. The name comes from an original wooden church built in the late 17th century during the reign of the Swedish King Charles XI. Although the church took 20 years to build, the large altar fresco was completed in ten days in 1879 by the well-known artist Johann Köler.

DOME CHURCH ↘ 644 4140; www.eelk.ee/tallinna.toom; open daily 09.00–17.00 [3 B5]

Work started on the Dome Church soon after the Danish invasion in the early 13th century and the first church was consecrated by King Waldemar II in 1240. It was slowly enlarged over the next four centuries as funds became available but much of the interior was destroyed in the fire of 1684 which devastated the whole of the Old Town. The Swedish King Charles XI imposed a special tax for the rebuilding of Tallinn and within two years the church had been largely restored. The Baroque spire was added in 1778 so in all the church has an architectural history of over 600 years. The altarpiece, painted in 1866, is the work of the Baltic-German artist Eduard von Gebhardt. The organ, probably the most powerful in Estonia, was made in Frankfurt an der Oder in 1913 and is the last to have been imported from Germany before World War I.

The Dome Church was the religious centre for the main families of the Tallinn Baltic-German community; their coats of arms cover the church walls and their tombstones cover the floor, although a few are of Swedish origin. At the back of the church are two tombstones commemorating the butchers' and the shoemakers' guilds. The most impressive tomb, which is beside the altar, is that of the French mercenary Pontus de la Gardie who served in the Swedish army in many battles with the Russians. In the north aisle is a monument to Samuel Greig, a Scottish admiral who served in the Tsarist navy from 1763 until his death in 1788. The inscription expresses the sorrow of Catherine II at his death. Like many Scottish predecessors and successors, he had a distinguished career in this navy. He helped to destroy the Turkish fleet at the Battle of Chesme in 1770 and to build up Kronstadt into a major naval base. Next to this monument is one to Adam von Krusenstern, the Baltic German who led the first Russian expedition to sail around the world, in 1803. Note the two globes, both of which omit New Zealand.

HOLY GHOST CHURCH ↘ 644 1487; www.eelk.ee/tallinna.puhavaimu; open daily 10.00–16.00 [2 C4]

That this church does not face due east suggests that there was already a complex street layout by 1300 when building began. It was the first church to hold services in Estonian and the first extracts from the catechism in the Estonian language were printed for use here in 1535. The pulpit is the original one dating from this time. Some of the panels along the balcony, under restoration from 2003, depict Old and New Testament themes, others the life of St Elizabeth of Thuringen, the patron saint of beggars and orphans. The 1684 fire destroyed much of the interior and the original spire but the next spire was for many years the oldest in Tallinn, dating from 1688. It was badly damaged in a fire in 2002 but was quickly replaced. Of the same age inside the church is the large wooden clock on the north wall, carved by Christian Ackermann from Königsberg. Spared from the fire was the folding altar carved in 1483 by the Lübeck artist Bernt Notke, whose *Dance Macabre* at Niguliste is noted below. Only the organ is modern, dating from 1929; it is one of the few in Tallinn's churches built by an Estonian and not imported from Germany. To the left of the altar, the White Ensign and the plaque below it commemorate the British sailors who gave their lives between 1918 and 1920 fighting the Bolsheviks.

A replica of this plaque was unveiled at Portsmouth Cathedral by Prince Andrew in December 2005.

ST MICHAEL'S SWEDISH CHURCH ✎ 644 1938; www.eelk.ee/tallinna.rootsi; open daily 10.00–18.00 [3 C5]
St Michael's does not have a tower as it was first built in the early 16th century as an almshouse and hospital. Only in the 18th century was it consecrated. The Swedish community all fled in 1944 which gave the Soviet authorities a pretext for converting the building into a sports centre, mainly used for boxing and wrestling. Generous support from the Swedish Lutheran community enabled it to be reconsecrated in 1993.

ST NICHOLAS'S CHURCH (NIGULISTE) ☎ *644 9911; www.ekm.ee; open Wed–Sun 10.00–18.00* [3 C5]

In common with many other Tallinn churches, St Nicholas's was first built in the 13th century and then expanded over the next 400 years. The original spire dated from 1696 and, being outside the town walls, the church was spared from the 1684 fire. It was, however, badly damaged during the Soviet air raid on Tallinn of 9 March 1944, having had its last service the day before. The spire was firmly restored only in 1984. An earlier replacement collapsed in 1982 and the Soviet authorities flooded the streets with police to stop photographs being taken of this humiliation. (They did not completely succeed.) The carvings, chandeliers and pictures, many dating from the 16th century, had fortunately been removed before the bombing. They are all now on display again and are particularly valuable given that so much similar work in Tallinn was either destroyed in the 1684 fire or suffered from neglect in more recent times. The silver collection suffered a more precarious fate, with much being looted during World War II, but with the addition of some donations, the current exhibition is a very representative collection of Estonian work in this field from the 15th century onwards.

The interior of the church was slowly restored during the Soviet period from 1953 onwards. A new exhibition was opened in 2005 which describes this work and captions are in English. St Nicholas's has kept its role as a museum and concert hall so has not been reconsecrated. The life of St Nicholas is portrayed in the altarpiece, over 6m wide and painted in Lübeck by Hermen Rode between 1478 and 1482. The *Dance Macabre* by Bernt Notke, another Lübeck artist, was painted a decade or so earlier and shows how nobody escapes death, whatever their powers when alive. Note the one very modern addition – a stained-glass window by the contemporary artist, Rait Prääts, whose glass can also be seen at the National Library and the Sakala Conference Centre.

ST OLAV'S CHURCH ↘ *641 2241; www.oleviste.ee; church open daily 10.00–14.00, tower open May–Sep 11.00–17.00* [2 C2]

When first built in 1267, St Olav's 140m-high steeple made it one of the tallest buildings in the world. This steeple caught fire in 1820, having been struck by lightning, and its replacement reaches 'only' 120m. It is still, however, a major feature of the Tallinn skyline and since the summer of 2002 has been open to the public. Much of the interior of the church was destroyed in the 1820 fire, as it had been in an earlier one in 1625. The rebuilding, completed in 1840, provides a contrast to most

St Olav's Church

other churches in Tallinn for its plain interior. Tsar Nicholas I donated a large bell in 1850 and his generosity is noted in an inscription written, with no trace of irony, in German. The organ dates from this time but the chandeliers are earlier and have been donated from other buildings.

PARKS AND GARDENS

Tallinn's solitary small park in the town centre, beside the Viru Hotel, was seriously under threat in 2005 and 2006 from the hotel's expansion plans. **Kadriorg Park**, however, remains safe, perhaps because the Presidential Palace (see page 134) is there.

KADRIORG PARK [1 D2]

A half-hour walk from the old town, Kadriorg Park is a year-round joy for local people and tourists alike. In winter the combination of sun and snow amidst the trees and sculptures offers a peaceful contrast to the hectic commercial life of Tallinn just a few hundred metres away. Spring brings out the blossom of the cherry and ash trees, summer the swans, the squirrels and the fountains and autumn the blends of gold and red as the trees shed their leaves.

The park brings together the local population as no other place does. Poor Russian-speakers from the grim estates further east may come here by bus to give their children some space to play. Richer Estonians will arrive early, before a concert or perhaps even a presidential reception, and sit beside the fountains. The arrival of KUMU (see page 129 [1 D2]), at the edge of the park, has no doubt increased visitors too and stimulated the removal of the few remaining Soviet buildings, which will be replaced by a café and tennis courts.

In the summer of 2006, the **Kadriorg Park Museum** (see page 143, [1 C3]) opened at Weizenbergi 26.

11 Beyond the City

Where Tallinn is keen to show either how medieval or how modern it is, trips outside will reveal an Estonia either still trapped in the Soviet period or much more content to return to nature. Ideally, add an extra day to a Tallinn visit to allow time for some of these very different experiences.

The two islands described, Aegna and Naissaar, can be visited only in the summer, but Rocca al Mare, Kadriorg and Pirita are equally attractive under snow. The former Soviet naval base at Paldiski is macabre all year round.

ROCCA AL MARE OPEN-AIR MUSEUM

Vabaõhumuuseumi tee 12; ℩ 654 9100; www.evm.ee; open May–Oct daily 10.00–18.00, although the buildings close at 16.00. Open Nov–Apr daily 10.00–17.00 but the buildings are closed then.

This museum deserves a half day to itself, ideally in balmy summer weather or after a heavy fall of snow. Take the number 21 or 21b bus from the railway station and also take a sweater as protection against the wind on the many non-balmy days. A winter excursion on a sunny day is worthwhile to get some impression of what most

157

Estonians used to endure month in, month out, every winter. Visitors at midsummer on 23/24 June can enjoy the all-night celebrations held here. The name in Italian means 'cliff beside the sea' and was given by the original owner of the estate when it was bought in 1863.

The museum was founded in 1957 and first opened to the public in 1964. The descriptive panels throughout are in English. It now consists of around 70 buildings and when complete should have 100. The aim is to show all aspects of Estonian rural architecture, with houses of both rich and poor. Most date from the 19th century but one of the chapels was built in 1699. The whole of Estonia is represented – windmills are, of course, from the island of Saaremaa but in contrast there are fishermen's cottages from Lake Peipsi on the Russian border. Even the poorest families managed to afford a sauna since to Estonians it is as crucial to living as a cooking pot. The interiors have all been appropriately furnished with kitchen utensils, weaving looms and chests of drawers.

Amongst the more unusual buildings is a tabernacle from the Herrnhut movement, a strict offshoot of the Lutheran Church. Future plans include the restoration of a Swedish cottage – about 8,000 Swedes lived in Estonia before World War II. There is already a Swedish church here, brought from the formerly Swedish-speaking village of Sutlepa. The exterior is 17th century and the interior 19th century. Inside there is a permanent exhibition of drawings from all the other Swedish churches in Estonia. In bad weather, finish your tour at the Kolu Tavern. Kolu is a village between Tallinn and Tartu, and the tavern here still has two separate bars, one originally for the gentry and one for the peasants. It serves filling, hot food such as pea soup and mashed potatoes with bacon, but do not expect any concessions to the 21st century; it remains firmly in the 19th, although a more conventional restaurant will in due course be built for more fastidious diners.

PALDISKI

Since independence, an uneasy quiet has descended on this former Soviet naval base situated 40km west of Tallinn. Unusually for Estonia, a regular train service operates from here to Tallinn, with eight services a day, the journey lasting a little over one hour. However, individual tourists would be well advised to take a car and guide for a half-day excursion as several en-route stops can be made. Estonians are more than happy to see the back of the Russian sailors but have yet to find a new role for this harbour. A daily car ferry service to Kappelskär in Sweden started in summer 2000 which provided much-needed employment and the switching of cargo services from Tallinn soon followed, which is helping to bring a sense of hope back into the town.

Peter the Great inspected the site personally in 1715 before authorising the building of a harbour which was originally planned as the largest in the Russian Empire and for defending the country against the Swedes. It was better protected than Tallinn and ice-free for much longer. This first point was brought home to Peter very forcefully in 1717 when two boats sank in a storm whilst moored in Tallinn harbour. From then until his death in 1825 he became obsessed with this project; the workforce was around 2,500 men supported by around 300 horses. A dam over 300m long was built. The harbour would never in fact be completed although innumerable attempts were made to do so in the 18th century. Much of the labour was supplied by prisoners; so many died of ill-treatment that Paldiski became known as the 'second Siberia'. The final straw came in 1757 when the workers' pay was reduced from two kopeks to one kopek a day and over 200 died of starvation in the months of March and April 1758 alone. The dam soon collapsed and what remained of the harbour was destroyed in a storm in 1818. Now only some of the fort remains.

In September 1939, the USSR imposed a mutual assistance pact on Estonia under which Paldiski was seized as a naval base. In May 1940, shortly before the full occupation of the country, all Estonians were expelled from the town, a practice that would be repeated all too often from 1945 in many other towns and villages along the coast. Paldiski is now the largest Soviet blot on the Estonian landscape; only the dustbins, brightly coloured and modelled on penguins with their beaks open, provide relief from piles of rubble, barbed wire and ransacked blocks of flats. Improvements are very slow to come here.

The first building to be seen on the way into the town is the former prison, but in the mid 1990s it could hardly be distinguished from much of what follows. When the Russian forces finally left in September 1995, having been granted dispensation to stay after independence, a population of around 4,000 was left with only 10% of them speaking Estonian; the remainder were Russian-speaking civilians. A curtain behind a window, an occasional light or even the sight of an occasional human being, showed that life has not totally died out here but the slogan in the town's English-language brochure, *A Town with a Future*, seemed at the time to be a joke in particularly bad taste. However, in 2000 a new hotel was opened, the **White Ship** (Valge Laev) at Rae 32 (✆ *674 2095; www.weekends.ee*). 'Welcome aboard' mats are behind each entrance, a porthole is on the door of every room and maritime memorabilia cover all the walls. It would be possible to commute into Tallinn from here, and when Tallinn hotels are full, late bookers will have no choice. The town should gradually benefit from Tallinn's property boom. Those unable to afford the capital itself started building and restoring here from around 2004, which can only lead to more colour and vitality throughout.

Returning to Tallinn, two very contrasting stops can be made. Shortly after independence, a monument was erected in the forest at **Klooga** to commemorate the massacre of 2,000 Jews there on 19 September 1944, just before the German withdrawal. The small Estonian-Jewish community had already been killed by then; these victims were largely from other eastern European countries. The former village of **Tabasalu** is now the first of Tallinn's suburbs, most of whose inhabitants have much more money than sense or taste. The money stands out, but it is well protected by high walls and Rottweilers. A few poultry farmers remain on the outskirts of the village but it cannot be long before they are bought out.

AROUND TALLINN BAY

Allow a full day to visit the island of Aegna, the yacht harbour at Pirita and the park at Kadriorg. Several buses serve Pirita from the town centre and the journey takes about ten minutes. The relevant bus stop is one beyond that for the hotel.

AEGNA Boats to and from Aegna operate out of Pirita harbour from a small jetty beside the café, not from the larger jetty beside the hotel and yacht club. Boats leave for the island around 09.00, at 12.00 and in the early evening. Services operate most years from mid June to mid September but check timings at the tourist office or via a hotel reception before setting off and do not forget an umbrella in case the weather suddenly changes. Prepare a picnic as well, since the kiosk at the harbour has a minimal supply of snacks. Tickets cost 80EEK (£3.50/US$5.50) for the round trip.

Aegna is so quiet that even Estonians are prepared to turn off their mobile phones, and neither the Germans nor the Russians were able to leave their mark. Conifer trees abound, as do minute beaches, and the few open areas have been made available for camping. Much of the island can be seen in the three hours allowed by the morning boat schedule though a full day of peace and quiet is what most local visitors seek. Paths are clearly marked and a detailed map is displayed at the harbour.

PIRITA, VIIMSI AND KADRIORG PALACE Pirita was built as the Olympic village for the yachting and sailing events of the 1980 Olympics. For a precious three weeks

162

Tallinn briefly returned to being an international city. An array of consumer goods, Western newspapers and direct international telephone dialling suddenly came to Tallinn and left equally suddenly when the games were over. Only the buildings have remained and they are so obviously of Soviet design that the harbour hardly seems to belong to modern Estonia. On returning to Pirita, visitors of Estonian origin may wish to take the number 34 bus for 2km inland to **Metsakalmistu**, the Forest Cemetery. Most famous Estonians are buried in this pine forest, including the writer A H Tammsaare, the poet Lydia Koidula and the chess player Paul Keres. They were joined in March 2006 by Estonia's president in the 1990s, Lennart Meri. Since independence, the body of Konstantin Päts, president until the Soviet occupation, has been returned and he is now buried here together with his immediate family. He died in a Soviet psychiatric hospital in 1956. The body of General Laidoner, however, still lies in 2001 in a communal grave in Vladimir Prison where he died in March 1953, despite strong pressure from the Estonian government for it to be formally identified and returned. His wife was released from prison in 1954 after his death but was allowed to return to Estonia only after her 70th birthday. She had been a pianist and took some music with her to Siberia, practising on walls and tables to keep her fingers fit. Johan Laidoner was commander-in-chief for much of the pre-war period and his former house on the Viimsi Peninsula, about 5km from Pirita, is now the **Laidoner Museum** (*Mõisa tee 1;* ℡ *621 7410; www.laidoner.ee; open Wed–Sun 11.00–18.00*). The most moving exhibit is a French–Russian dictionary given to him during his imprisonment in 1944; he used several pages of it to compose his political testament. It ends, in English, with the words 'Estonia, with all thy faults, I love thee still. Johan Laidoner'. Considering how jealous Stalin was of his reputation, it is remarkable how many items associated with him and with this house have survived. During Soviet times the KGB had taken it over in order to break completely the links with Estonian independence. Estonians are pleased to point out that Laidoner did in the end outlive Stalin, even if only by a few days in March 1953.

The museum was greatly expanded in 2001 and again in 2003. With the help of the Imperial War Museum in London there is now a British Room, covering the navy's role in helping to establish Estonian independence in 1918–20. There are two memorials to this, one in the Holy Ghost Church in Tallinn (see page 152), and one in Portsmouth Cathedral. Both were unveiled by Prince Andrew. It is expected that many more exhibits will soon come from Britain. This would be appropriate in view of Laidoner's often-quoted remark 'Without the arrival of the British fleet in Tallinn in December 1918, Estonia and the other Baltic states would have found themselves in the hands of the Bolsheviks.' The Poles have likewise opened a room in honour of Marshal Pilsudski who played a similar role to Laidoner in ensuring his country's independence from Russia.

The walk back to the centre of Tallinn is two or three miles. Cross the main road from the harbour to the site of **St Birgitta's Convent**. Although the convent is included in most sightseeing tours, walking here can be a precarious experience as the surroundings of the ruin are so badly maintained. The convent lasted intact for only 170 years, from 1407 until the siege of 1577 when it was largely destroyed by troops of Ivan IV in the Livonian Wars. The outline of the main body of the church is clear; the western gable together with the vestry, cloister and refectories can be identified. Minor restoration and excavation work started in 1960 and was brought to a close only in 2001. The new convent on the north side was completed in 2000 and part of the building is used as a hotel (see page 69).

St Birgitta's Convent

Turning back towards Tallinn, the buildings along the coast all date from the late 1970s, when they were built for the 1980 Olympic Games. Most events, of course, took place in Moscow that year, but Tallinn competed successfully with Leningrad and Sochi for the sailing events: the Olympic flame burned on this site from 20 to 30 July 1980. Soviet publications of the time report on the enthusiastic participation of 200,000 'volunteers' who ensured the project was completed on time – in fact, a full month ahead of the games starting. One pensioner apparently worked here without pay for 5,025 hours and earned 22 gold badges as a result. The road from Tallinn was widened into a dual carriageway as part of the preparations for the Olympics, and the site of the games now functions as a yacht harbour and a hotel complex.

Close to the Tallinn side of the harbour, shortly after the road again joins the coast, there are two monuments between the road and the sea. Linger in this area for the views across the bay of both old Tallinn and the new financial centre. One of the monuments was unveiled on 12 September 1989, the 100th anniversary of the tragic parachute jump undertaken by Charles Leroux. He had 238 successful jumps behind him but on this occasion was blown out to sea and drowned. The monument is the work of Estonia's most famous sculptor, Mati Karmin, who was born in 1959. His career, therefore, spans both the Soviet and the independence periods. Amongst his many famous works are the Kissing Students in Tartu Town Hall Square and the memorial on Hiiumaa Island to those killed on the Estonia in September 1994. The smaller memorial is to Michael Park, co-driver to the Estonian rally driver Markko Martin. Park was killed in a crash, which Martin survived, in September 2005 at a rally in Wales.

Staying on the land side of the main road, after half a mile is the **Soviet War Memorial**. It could hardly be anything else, given its size and the military themes of the bronze statues. The Estonians carry out minimal maintenance here but, as with all Soviet war memorials, they are not removed and Russians congregate on the days of the old Soviet holidays such as May Day and 7 November. The text is particularly offensive to Estonians as the monument is dedicated to 'Fighters for Soviet Power'. It was completed only in 1975. A Soviet guidebook excuses this long delay by claiming 'at last Estonian artists had enough skill and adequate economic means to complete such an ensemble'. The obelisk dates from 1960 and commemorates the hurried departure from Tallinn of the Bolshevik fleet in 1918 when German forces occupied the town.

An even more dominant landmark from the Soviet era is the **TV Tower** (↘ 623 8250; www.teletorn.ee; open daily 10.00–midnight) about a mile inland from Pirita on

Kloostrimetsa. Going there by bus, expect to be surrounded by elderly Russians with flowers since the Russian cemetery and crematorium are nearby. The few tourists who now visit the tower also seem to be Russian. This is a pity as it does provide an extensive view of the town and port not available elsewhere. The entrance is as flamboyant as one would expect; the windows are of stained glass, with portraits of valiant industrial workers; covered aisles surround basins of fountains which in turn are surrounded by lawns. However, nothing has been maintained properly (except for the lifts inside) so moss and weeds become ever more prominent. Nobody has bothered to put Estonian signs in the lift or change the menu in the revolving tower restaurant from smoked fish and chicken Kiev. The telescope still takes kopek coins. However prices are almost as dated too; it is many years since liqueurs in central Tallinn cost only 30EEK a glass.

A few hundred yards further along this road is **Maarjamäe Palace** (*Pirita tee 56;* ↘ *621 7410; www.eam.ee; open Wed–Sun 11.00–18.00*) [1 E1], which has probably had one of the most turbulent ownership histories of any site in Tallinn. Maarjamäe means 'Mary's Hill' but the German name, Streitberg ('Hill of Strife'), was for many centuries more appropriate. The only consolation is that the blood shed here spared Tallinn itself from many battles. The final one took place in the early 18th century as Russia seized the Baltics from the Swedes during the Northern Wars. To set the seal on his conquest, Peter the Great established Kadriorg Park as a summer residence, so many of the St Petersburg nobility felt obliged to follow suit. Those who could not immediately afford the luxury of a suitable building subsidised it with a factory, so lime kilns and sugar refineries adjoined the manor houses. The sugar was sold in Riga and St Petersburg and the plant was run on British coal. A fire in 1868 destroyed much of the factory and it was never rebuilt. In the 1870s, when the estate was bought by Count Anatoli Orlov-Davydov from St Petersburg, the rebuilding he ordered came to deserve the title 'palace'. Terraces, a gateway decorated with copper eagles and the Gothic tower gave it an almost regal air. The Dutch consulate bought it in the 1920s when the Orlov-Davydovs emigrated to France, and continued its use as a summer residence. It was to lose its appeal in this role when in 1926 the road to Pirita was built across the grounds, cutting off the manor house from direct and private access to the sea. However, the road brought with it commercial potential which was eventually realised in a hotel and restaurant called the Riviera Palace. In 1937, the Estonian air force took it over as a training school and they are sadly responsible for its dreary façade. From 1940 until 1975, when Maarjamäe became a museum, the Soviet military used but did not abuse it. During the 1980s, Polish restorers finally brought the building back to its turn-of-the-century glory, turning their attention to the chandeliers, fireplaces, parquet floors and ceilings. It is ironic that one of the last Soviet legacies to Tallinn should be the perfect surroundings for a museum which chronicles Estonian independence.

Although few labels are in English and the one available guidebook is now badly out of date, this is without doubt the best museum in Tallinn. New rooms are constantly being added, exhibits are generously displayed, the layout is sensibly planned and there is the complete absence of benign neglect that seems to permeate so many other Tallinn museums. It covers Estonian history from the mid 19th century until the present day. It amply contrasts the lifestyles of rich and poor and shows the diversity of industrial products and international contacts that the country enjoyed during the first period of independence between the two world wars. It even had a thriving tourist board whose brochures displayed here sold Estonia as 'The Cheapest and Most Interesting Country in Europe'. One room opened in the summer of 1998 is devoted to the life of Konstantin Päts, Estonia's president between the two World Wars.

It features portraits both of his close political associates and of his main opponents, as well as all the work of Ants Laikmaa, the most famous Estonian artist of that time. That their dates of death are nearly all 1940 or 1941 shows the brutality of the Soviet occupation. A room dedicated to the Forest Brothers, the guerrilla organisation that fought the Soviet occupation in the late 1940s, covers this theme movingly but not bombastically. The role of Estonians living in St Petersburg is often forgotten but the museum covers a demonstration held there by 40,000 of them in March 1917; this demonstration played a crucial role in the build-up to independence.

What to do with the conference room at the museum is clearly a topic of embarrassment. Its wall mural, 'Peoples' Friendship', was completed in 1987 by one of the most famous artists of the Soviet era, Evald Okas, so it just preceded perestroika and then independence. Visitors who wander in will find it totally curtained, but there is no objection from the staff to drawing back the curtains to view it.

At the back of the museum are some Soviet statues too big (and too boring) to drag to the Occupation Museum in the town centre. For many years these were all in a cluster on the ground and most were broken. However a relatively intact Lenin was standing up in the summer of 2006 looking down on all his fallen successors.

Continuing towards the town centre is one of the few late1950s constructions of which Estonians can be fiercely proud – the **Song Festival Amphitheatre** [1 D2]. It has the massive grandeur to be expected from that time but is not wasteful of materials and does not dominate the surrounding area. The parabola provides cover for 5,000 singers and up to 20,000 more have often taken part. The most famous recent festival took place in 1989, when the previously banned national anthem, *My Native Land*, was sung by an audience of around 300,000 people, 20% of the entire population of the country. In winter, the steep slope at the back of the parabola provides Tallinn's only ski- and toboggan-run. Note the plaques at the top of the slope which commemorate each of the Song Festivals held every five years since 1869. The 2004 festival was commemorated by a statue at the top of the auditorium to Gustav Ernesaks (1908–93) who did more than anyone else to keep the Estonian element alive in the Song Festivals held during Soviet times. The tower was opened to the public in 2000 and gives photographers good shots of the Old Town and the port combined.

Returning to the shoreline, at the junction of the roads to Pirita and to Narva, note the **Russalka (Mermaid) Memorial** [1 D2], which commemorates the sinking of a battleship with this name in 1893. It depicts an angel looking out to sea. In 2005, replica gas lamps were installed around the monument. Do not be surprised to see Russian-speaking wedding couples laying flowers here on a Saturday. The sculptor, Amandus Adamson, is one of Estonia's most famous, and perhaps because of this monument he was granted official respect in the Soviet period and a memorial bronze bust of him stands in Kadriorg Park – one corner of which is just behind the Russalka Memorial.

Inland, the vista is now dominated by **KUMU** [1 D3] which well deserves all four capital letters, given the size of the building. It looks down from the hill at the eastern end of Kadriorg Park [1 D2]. This is the **Eesti Kunstimuuseum** (*www.kumu.ee*); see page 129, the Estonian Art Museum, which opened in February 2006. Everything is 'big' about it; even the lift holds 122 people. A small selection of the art shown here came from the Knighthood Building on Toompea where it had been on temporary display since 1992 but much is now shown for the first time, including a collection dedicated to the Soviet period. The atmosphere is totally different from that in the cramped buildings of the Old Town; there has finally been some outreach to the many people who feel intimidated from entering other museums in Estonia. In its first two months, over 1,000 people a day visited KUMU, an amazing figure for a Baltics museum out of the tourist season. Cafés, a children's centre and an auditorium have all helped in this endeavour, as will regular temporary exhibitions by contemporary artists.

Kadriorg Park (see page 156), and **Kadriorg Palace** (see page 134 [1 D2]) which forms its centrepiece, are the next stage of the walk, attracting locals and visitors alike.

Around 100m back towards town, on Weizenbergi opposite the main entrance to Kadriorg Palace, the **Mikkel Museum** (see page 139 [1 D3]), once the palace kitchen, now houses an eclectic art collection. On leaving the museum and turning left, a slight detour to the far side of the lake, behind the Mikkel building, takes you to the splendidly isolated **Eduard Vilde House Museum** (see page 128) at Roheline 3.

To continue back into town, return to Weizenbergi.

At the corner of Poska on the left, house number 20a has some Baroque imitation of the palace although it was built only in 1939. Weizenbergi lasts a further 300m or so before joining Narva mnt. Each house is probably now owned, or was before World War II, by a famous Estonian. Ladas or small Toyotas may be parked in the street, but considerable wealth is discreetly hidden behind the lace curtains. The turn-of-the-century, four-storey houses display hints of Jugendstil, whilst the wooden ones are characteristic of middle-class suburbs throughout Estonia. On a neighbouring street, Koidula, one of the largest wooden houses belonged to Estonia's most famous author, A H Tammsaare, who died in March 1940, see page 146 for details. In his honour it is now the **Tammsaare Museum**.

At the junction of Weizenbergi and Narva mnt there is a taxi rank and bus stop. A large Methodist church has recently been built on the far side; otherwise Narva mnt from here back to the Viru Gate is totally devoted to Mammon. There is no point in describing any of the buildings since they are mainly being pulled down to give way to glass skyscrapers. This area will soon be Tallinn's Wall Street or Square Mile. A Japanese restaurant has already opened to ensure a serious and affluent gastronomic ambience.

NAISSAAR

If Tallinn is cutting edge, dynamic and every other cliché associated with the capitals of the EU accession countries, the island of Naissaar is the complete opposite. Its website remains only in Estonian and its boat schedules a state secret until the service starts sometime in early summer. Sometimes a day trip is possible; sometimes schedules require an overnight stay in one of the cottages adapted into hostels. The boat goes from the same jetty just beyond Pirita that is used by the Aegna boat. The electricity supply, usually limited to two hours in the morning and two in the evening, imposes a firm schedule for going to bed and for getting up. Visitors are not allowed to bring alcohol with them but there is one café that can supply the modest needs in this field of most visitors. Yet those who take a four-hour walking tour will be amply rewarded by seeing the legacies not only of those who lived there but also of those who succeeded in occupying the island, as well as those who, like the British navy, just dropped by for a few months. It is advisable to pre-book a guide, if only to be sure of avoiding areas where there could still be unexploded mines, the worst of several Soviet legacies.

Naissaar has had to reinvent itself several times during the 250 years since it began to be regularly inhabited. The name means 'women's island' but there is no clear origin for this name, only fanciful and largely unprintable legends. Ironically, it has in fact been male-dominated for most of its occupation with women having far less importance than on the mainland. The early Swedish-speaking settlers who

11

came in the mid 18th century were fishermen who traded their catches and spruce in Tallinn for the agricultural goods that the sandy windswept terrain on the island did not allow them to grow. Many in fact had lived in Finland and they came to escape the Tsarist seizure of Finland from the Swedes. Naissaar was free from plague then and also free from Baltic-German landlords, which encouraged a community of around 200–300 to settle there; the population stayed around this level until World War II. A Swedish primary school was established in 1874 and an Estonian one in 1925. In winter, the island was always cut off for several weeks at a time when the ice was too thick for the boats to secure a passage, but too thin for horses or, later, cars to cross. The few affluent islanders were invariably pilots who guided foreign trading ships into Tallinn harbour. Captains unwilling to pay their fees could find their boats shipwrecked around Naissaar and the cargoes that were salvaged provided a useful addition to income from fishing. In 1854, the British navy occupied the island for a few months as part of its attempt to blockade supplies from reaching Russia during the Crimean War. This was long enough for them to show the islanders how to play cricket, but the game did not catch on.

The population was first deported by the Russians in 1730 when they built a fortress to defend the island from possible Swedish attacks. There would be three further deportations by the Russians in the 20th century. The first occasion was in 1914 as the Tsarist armies tried to defend it from the Germans. The second was in 1940 at the start of the first Soviet occupation. Residents were assured that they would not have to pay for transport to the mainland and were invited to pass on any special wishes to the authorities. The third deportation was in 1944 when the Soviets returned after the Germans had retreated to Latvia. It would be 50 years before any Estonian could live there again.

Visitors are likely to stay in the village of **Männiku**, about 2km from the port, where the island administrative centre and café are based. The houses look reasonably modern but very un-Soviet with the use of light woods and extensive glass. This is because they were all prefabricated in Finland and were part of the reparations demanded by the Soviet Union from Finland at the end of World War II. The larger Soviet buildings, including the factory that produced the mines, have all been abandoned but a schoolroom has been converted into an amusing museum. Much has been left as the Russians abandoned it, with posters proclaiming perestroika, unread books by Lenin and enormous radiograms. Two waxworks have been added of Soviet marines, one asleep and one on the toilet. The narrow-gauge railway ends here and can sometimes be taken for a ride back to the port.

The now abandoned village of **Lõunaküla** is on the southern shore of the island and until World War II was its centre. Not a single house now remains from that time. The shell of the church is from one built in 1934 by the Swedish Lutheran Church. It replaced an earlier one built in 1856 but burnt down by the Bolsheviks during their brief occupation of the island in 1918. The **cemetery** built beside the shore contains the graves of sailors who died not in battle on the island but at sea. It was not built beside the church since the Catholic French soldiers could not be buried on Lutheran ground.

In the middle of 2006 it looked as though Naissaar might finally be getting a new lease of life, at least during the summer. Estonia's most famous impresario/conductor, Tõnu Kaljuste, began a series of musical events on the island, with special boats before and after the concerts. These were sold out well in advance throughout the season so there is likely to be a wide range of concerts again in summer 2007. Further information will be available on his website www.tonukaljuste.ee or that of Naissaar Island www.naissaar.ee, although the latter has very little information in English.

LAHEMAA NATIONAL PARK

Situated along the north coast of Estonia, about 100km from Tallinn en route to Narva, Lahemaa National Park and the buildings within it show both the Baltic-German and the Soviet occupations at their most benevolent. The von der Pahlen family, which owned Palmse Mansion, the architectural high point of a visit to the park, contributed to Estonia for two centuries with their administrative, commercial and academic activities. Whilst to the west, the Soviets would blight the outskirts of Tallinn with shoddy tower blocks and to the east ransack the coast with oil-shale exploitation, Lahemaa, the Land of Bays, was given the status of a protected national park in 1971 and great efforts were made to support and enhance the wildlife of the area. Similar support was given to restoration of the manor houses and fishing villages. The boundaries of the park stretch for 40km along the coast and include several islands. Most Estonians, and all foreigners, were forbidden to enter the park because of its proximity to the coast but this did at least prevent any tourist and industrial development. Building work is now restricted to the minimum necessary to grant access to visitors and to provide for their stay.

GETTING THERE Within a full day, it is possible to cover most sights and return to Tallinn the same day. The website (*www.lahema.ee*) has full details of the opening hours of the different houses and transport links in the area. Given the distances between the major sites, hiring a car or joining a group tour is the best way to travel around the park. Group tours are arranged by local tour operators (see page 47). Taking a taxi is also surprisingly reasonable. A bus service operates twice daily from Tallinn to Palmse and Sagadi, and more frequently to Võsu and Viitna. There is also a twice-daily bus service from Haljala into the park. Many of the buses going east from Tallinn to Narva stop at Viitna and Haljala. A limited bus service operates within the park, but stops are always conveniently situated close to the manor houses or in the village centres. Cyclists can bring their bikes on the many public buses that link the villages of Võsu, Käsmu and Palmse with Tallinn and Rakvere. The company Citybike (*www.citybike.ee*) arranges tours from Tallinn with transportation to and fro, with the day spent in the park.

TOURING THE PARK Leave the St Petersburg Highway from Tallinn to Narva at Viitna and then drive through Palmse, Sagadi, Altja, Võsu, Käsmu, Viinistu and Kolga before returning to the main road 18km further west. Drivers starting from the east or south will come off the main road at Haljala and begin the tour at Sagadi. Viitna is best known for its coaching inn, which dates from 1791. Like so many buildings in Estonia, it was destroyed at some stage in its history by fire; what is surprising is that the fire here was in 1989. Let us hope that it is the last serious fire to blight Estonian architecture. The inn appeals most in midwinter with its open fire and substantial portions of food, but at all times of year offers a good respite from the dull drive between Tallinn and the Russian border at Narva. It is no longer a hotel, but in the days of horse-drawn transport it served this function, being a day's ride from Tallinn. The inn was clearly divided into two sections so that masters and servants would not eat together.

PALMSE MANOR The manor is 6km off the main road, the perfect distance to ensure easy access but equally to ensure a totally calm natural environment. It is without doubt the most impressive manor house in Estonia and the 15 years of restoration between 1971 and 1986 have left a lasting and appropriate memorial to the von der Pahlen family. The main building and the surrounding gardens were begun in 1697 but the Northern War between Sweden and Russia halted construction. It was completed in 1740 and then work started on the other buildings. The family lived here until 1923, when the estate was nationalised in accordance with the Land Law of 1919. The land was then divided amongst ten families and the house became a convalescent home; after World War II the Soviet administration converted it into a pioneer camp for young people. The other buildings had all been left to decline and by 1971, when restoration began, were in such poor condition that it was necessary to consult drawings and photographs from the turn of the century to see their original format. Different histories like to typecast both the architecture of the manor house and the landscaping of the gardens. The former has been labelled French, Dutch and Italian, the latter English and Chinese. None of these is helpful as the von

Palmse Manor

der Pahlens wanted a tasteful, solid and modest environment both indoors and outdoors and used largely local materials. They had no desire or need for ostentation as they all had highly successful careers in many different fields. They distilled as profitably as they ran the Baltic Railway Company; their paintings are as worthy as their botanical research. Apart from one episode in 1805, their 200-year rule passed without peasant unrest and the famous Estonian writer of the 19th century, Friedrich Reinhold Kreutzwald, puts this down to the relationship between the family and their farmers being similar to that between parents and children. They shunned military activity and the only sign of Prussian patriotism is the name they gave in 1871 to one of the paths through the wood – Parisian Way – following the defeat of the French by the Prussian army the previous year.

Apart from one chair in the main bedroom, and the chandelier in the reception, none of the furniture is original but the items that have been collected from all over Estonia are similar to those the family would have used. The chairs in the concert hall have all been recently produced, but follow the original designs. The late 19th-century music box is still in working order and plays 24 different pieces, mainly dance music. The drawings and charts on the first floor are by the 20th-century artist Olev Soans (1925–95) although many are modelled on 19th-century originals. On the balustrade are two monograms, one from the von der Pahlen family in 1785 and one added 200 years later to commemorate the restoration in 1985. The tiled stoves throughout the house are original, as are the two granite obelisks that guard the entrance. To the left of the main building is a small wooden one which looks like a small chapel. It has the German name 'Kavalierhaus', which defies translation into English but was where the younger people congregated. Now it would be a computer centre by day and a disco by night but, in the early 19th century, sedate dancing could take place for much of the day. Its current use is as a discreet souvenir shop. To the right, behind the main building, is the former bath house, which has now been converted into a café.

In the former stables in front of the café, there is now a transport museum with an exhibition of cars, bicycles and motorbikes, some of which date back to the 1930s. The most notable items are a fire engine sent from Viljandi to Tallinn in March 1944 to help deal with the aftermath of the Soviet bombing, and the Zil that belonged to Alexandra Kollontai, a close associate of Lenin in the run-up to the 1917 revolution but who was then exiled into the diplomatic corps by Stalin.

Further left is the orchard and the greenhouse, testimony to several generations of botanists in the family. Sadly the greenhouse no longer cultivates the plums, apricots and pineapples which used to enhance the family meals. The distillery has been converted into a hotel and although it serves a wide range of Estonian spirits, none is now produced within the confines of the park. The former stables are now an information centre for the whole park and the shop there sells a wider range of maps and guides than does the souvenir shop. Particularly useful in this respect are two leaflets, *Viru Bog Nature Trail* and *Lahemaa Birds*. A walk along the lakeside is worthwhile, if only for the view back to the main house, but it can then be extended by taking one of the many different trails through the woods. Of sociological rather than architectural interest is the monument to the von der Pahlens erected in 1933 by the ten families who took over their land which shows the affection with which they were still regarded a decade after their departure. More impressive, although untouched by humans, are the erratic boulders, the massive lumps of granite that cluster in several places in the woods.

SAGADI Sagadi is a 6km drive from Palmse and its manor house is very different. Local writers prefer it to Palmse, making comparisons with the chateaux on the Loire and even with the Garden of Eden. Travellers arriving with such expectations will definitely be disappointed, but those with a more open mind will see how a typical Baltic-German family lived and ruled. The land was owned by the von Fock family from the 17th century, but the current building, and those immediately surrounding it, date largely from the 1750s. Construction was not therefore hindered by the Northern War, which halted work at Palmse. The façade was rebuilt in 1795, with the addition of the balcony. The von Focks had a variety of business careers, largely in shipbuilding and in forestry, but none reached the eminence of the von der Pahlens. The family lived in the building until 1939 although, following the Land Law of 1919, the estates were nationalised and the main building became a primary school. It kept this function until 1970, and soon afterwards full restoration of the whole estate began. Some of the furniture is original but, as at Palmse, many pieces have been brought from other houses that were not restored. The carpet in the banqueting hall is from Aubusson in France and belonged to President Konstantin Päts. The Forestry Museum used to be in the main house, but has recently been extended and is now in an annexe. Some labels are in English. The craft shops in the former stables offer a wide selection of souvenirs at prices much lower than those charged by shops in Tallinn.

ALTJA The fishing village of Altja is 8km from Sagadi. It has never been much more than a hamlet but it suffered under the Soviet regime when fishing, its sole livelihood, was banned and the population dropped from around 120 down to merely 20. Subsistence farming was hardly a substitute as only potatoes could grow in the sandy soil and the grazing lands supported only a minimal number of cattle or oxen. Fishing is now being revived and the excellent inn, which tourist groups use, provides employment during the summer. Although outsiders, even Estonians, were not allowed access to the coast at that time, restoration of the wooden buildings started in 1971. The inn dates from the early 19th century and, for most of its life, women were not admitted except on 25 March, Lady Day. Most of the buildings are not in fact inhabited but are netsheds for storing boats and fishing equipment. There are several walks along the coast, and paths have been cleared between the erratic boulders. Given the isolation and, in the winter, the desolation of this village, it is hard to picture it 100 years ago as an affluent port where the fishermen and boat builders could enjoy coffee and wine.

VÕSU Eighteen kilometres to the west lies the seaside resort of Võsu, popular throughout the summer with Estonian families. It was quite a grand resort in the 19th century but has since broadened its appeal, families in the 1920s coming here by ferry from Tallinn. Yet it is never overcrowded and the pine woods that back on to the beach make for pleasant short walks both in the summer and on a bright winter's day in the snow. Well into the 21st century one of the last functioning Soviet canteens could be tracked down opposite the Mere Hotel. It did not have a name so was simply called Soogisaal ('eating hall') and perhaps because of the little available choice nearby, it survived. It was finally brought into modern Estonia in 2005.

KÄSMU The village of Käsmu is a further 8km along the coast. When built in the early 19th century, it was often known as 'millionaire's village', such were the profits made from salt smuggling. In the 1920s smuggling shifted to alcohol when Finland attempted to impose prohibition. Finland gave up this aim in April 1932 and Käsmu suffered considerably. A macabre end to this traditional role came in June 1940 when many likely victims of Soviet hostility were smuggled out of Estonia before the whole country was occupied.

Käsmu is clearly no ordinary fishing village and this early prosperity shows signs of returning as affluent Tallinn businessmen buy up the former captains' houses. The main building is the Maritime Museum which previously served as a navigation college during the first period of independence and then as a coastguard station in the Soviet period. The large watchtower beside the building of course dates from the latter, when swimming was banned after 21.00, such was the supposed risk that escapes to Finland might be made under the cover of darkness. The museum has two unique features in that there is no admission charge and it is open at any time. The owner, Aarne Vaik, spent 20 years collecting material surreptitiously for the museum when there was no chance of displaying it. At present the collection concentrates on the 1920s and 1930s but it will eventually be extended through World War II and the Soviet period. A natural history section to cover sea fauna and flora is also being planned. One item of particular interest to British tourists is the £1 note from 1919; with all local currencies at that time being so insecure, sterling was the only acceptable currency for maritime insurance.

Beside the village church is the Baron Dellingshausen Memorial, perhaps unique in being built by him to feign his death. He was implicated in the failed plot to kill Tsar Alexander II in 1881 and fled to Germany with this memorial as a safeguard against the police looking for him. The false tomb was soon discovered but the baron was able to die of natural causes in the safe environment of Potsdam. The building now houses a photographic exhibition of local people at work and at home, all the pictures having been taken in 1999.

VIINISTU Visitors who turned up in this village during the 1990s would have found a village that modern Estonia had completely ignored. Thanks though to a former manager of Abba, the successful Swedish pop group, it has suddenly become mainstream.

Jaan Manitski, who was born here in 1943, could chart his family links to the area stretching back 400 years, so when the family fled to Sweden in 1944, they always hoped to return. He did so in 1989 when, having made a fortune, he decided that money was no longer of great importance to him. He compared it to cow dung: something useful in small doses but which stinks in larger quantities. His first work in Viinistu was growing mushrooms; he then had a short spell as Estonian foreign minister where he caused havoc in the accounts department when he left by not bothering to claim his last month's salary. He is now part-owner of Estonia's major daily paper *Eesti Päevaleht* but what he will definitely be remembered for is the Viinistu Art Museum, which opened in 2003.

Until 2006, visitors were rewarded with the best collection of 20th-century Estonian art in the whole country, and in particular with works by Konrad Mägi (1878–1925) and Eduard Viiralt (1898–1954). Obviously KUMU in Tallinn now exhibits more, but this should not deter visitors from coming here as well. The

11

collection is being extended and several rooms are devoted to temporary exhibitions, some of which will undoubtedly shock more sensitive visitors, who may prefer to limit their viewing to the permanent collection. The building is beside the sea; a concert hall and hotel were built nearby in 2004. More buildings are added each year and details of recent developments are on the website (*www.viinistukunst.ee*). Rich Estonians who patronise the arts are very rare; as more businesspeople enjoy the success that Jaan Manitski did, let us hope they follow in his footsteps.

KOLGA Kolga is 30km west of Käsmu so can be visited on the way back to Tallinn. The estate was originally a monastery, but in 1581 the Swedish king gave it to his French army commander Pontus de la Gardie as a reward for his military prowess. He himself hardly used it as he was drowned in the Narva River four years later in 1585, but the property stayed in his family until the mid 17th century when Christina de la Gardie married the Swedish Admiral Otto Stenbock. The 'Stenbock era' was to last until 1940 when the family returned to Sweden at the time of the Soviet occupation, but few senior members of the family ever really used it. Eric Stenbock, who spent a year here in 1886–87, was perhaps the most colourful member of the family to come. He had hoped to marry and settle in the house, but having failed in this endeavour, he returned to Sweden, though is remembered for the quantities of opium which he smoked there and for the games of charades that he organised for local children.

The estate was then inevitably allowed to degenerate and only in 1980 did maintenance and restoration begin. Much remains to be done but a visit is still worthwhile as it is easy to picture how impressive the whole area must have been. The classical columns surmounted by the Stenbock coat of arms were built at the turn of the 18th and 19th centuries when the family was at its most prosperous, thanks to its successful distilling and farming. It is to be hoped that such prosperity quickly returns to the area.

DAY TRIP TO HELSINKI *Nigel Wallis*

Founded in 1510 by King Gustav of Sweden, Helsinki's original *raison d'être* was to rival Tallinn in the battle for Baltic trade at a time when Tallinn was firmly in Russian hands. Some 500 years later and it's the tourist trade which tops the agenda, with numerous high-speed ferry crossings ready to whisk you the 80km across the Gulf of Finland in around 90 minutes.

Helsinki's charm for the day tripper lies in its compactness. Despite a population that nudges one million, twice that of Tallinn, boats dock in the heart of the city and within five minutes you can be admiring opulent Russian architecture, browsing über-chic boutiques or strolling through leafy parks. Most major attractions can be reached on foot and, whilst you won't see everything, a single day is sufficient to whet the appetite.

The long, warm days of summer see Helsinkiites unwinding in the many parks and terrace cafés. Either on the beach or island hopping around the archipelago, it's hard to believe you're in one of Europe's northernmost capitals. Winter brings a unique, magical air. Blanketed by snow, the city surreally expands as the sea freezes over and people venture across the ice. Muffled against the icy chill, in these months the warm museums and steamy cafés seem all the more inviting. But ultimately, whatever the time of year, one day may not be enough.

For more information on getting to Helsinki from Tallinn, see page 32.

EATING AND DRINKING With everything from Michelin-starred restaurants to the ritualistic late-night hot-dog stand, you won't starve in Helsinki. Classic institutions are the grand old *kahvilas* (cafés), where you can indulge in Finland's true passion – not sauna, but *kahvi* (coffee). Finns drink around five cups each per day, and these places are part of the city's heritage. They also serve up a cholesterol-packing, waistband-popping array of cakes and pastries, together with tasty salads and warm main dishes. For a true taste of Helsinki life, try the following.

✗ **Café Esplanad** Pohjoisesplanadi 37; ✆ 665 496. I came here for the first time in the depths of winter when chattering in from a snowstorm to a wonderland of sweet-smelling delights. Have no doubt, Café Esplanad has some of the most colossal cakes and pastries you could ever hope to see. Succumb to a monstrous meringue; you can walk it off later. *Sandwiches and desserts* €8.00–10.00; open 09.00–22.00.

✗ **Café Strindberg** Pohjoisesplanadi 33; ✆ 681 2030. Next door to Café Esplanad is one of the most stylish places to take your *kahvi* – the summer terrace in the park is an ideal people-watching haunt. Finnish specialities such as Baltic herring and reindeer fillet feature heavily on the bistro menu. Round it all off with a mouthwatering blueberry clafoutis. Set *lunch* € 7.00–19.00; *open* 09.00–22.00.

✗ **Fazer** Kluuvikatu 3; ✆ 729 6702. The main outlet of the Fazer confectionery brand, opened in 1891, exudes an opulent grandeur and relaxed demeanour that means hours can pass like minutes. Their delicious chocolate rivals anything you can get elsewhere. *Sandwiches* € 6.90–8, *salads* € 11.50–12, *warm dishes* € 16.50–19. *Open Mon–Sat 09.00–22.00.*

One of Helsinki's finest market experiences awaits as you disembark the ferry, so why not eat on the run or assemble a lip-smacking picnic?

✗ **Kauppatori and Kauppahalli** Eteläranta and Pohjoisesplanadi. Locals love the *kauppatori* (fish market) and *kauppahalli* (indoor market), and why not? Fish such as herring and perch, fresh from the boats, tempt the dawn punters who chat over the obligatory coffee. Wafts of smoked ham and reindeer are hard to miss, whilst summer berries add vivid colour (lingonberries and cloudberries are particular favourites). Inside the *kauppahalli* fresh bread and mounds of sticky pastries lie in wait. For a real fast-food treat, sniff out a local pancake stall. *Open Mon–Fri 08.00–18.00, Sat 0800–16.00.*

WHAT TO SEE AND DO Disembark the ferry and browse the **Kauppatori** and **Kauppahalli** (see above) before taking a moment to inspect your surroundings. To the north is the **Presidential Palace**, where behind the imposing columns of the façade Tarja Kaarina Halonen, Finland's current (and first female) president, conducts her official business.

From the boat you'll have noticed two major landmarks. A short eastward walk brings you to the Byzantine majesty of the **Uspensky Cathedral**, perhaps the ultimate legacy of Helsinki's Russian past. Consecrated in 1868, this is the largest Orthodox church in western Europe – even on the gloomiest February day the gilt onion domes radiate a warming glow. Head back west along Aleksanterinkatu to **Senaatintori** (Senate Square) and the green domes of **Tuomiokirkko** (Helsinki Cathedral), designed by C L Engel and dating from 1852. Many other fine Engel works, including the University Library and the Council of State, can be found by the cathedral.

Turning left down Unioninkatu, you emerge at the **tourist office** on Pohjoisesplanadi. In front of you is **Esplanad Park**, a wide tree-lined avenue and a major artery in Helsinki's cultural scene. Head north along Pohjoisesplanadi past a swathe of designer shops and classic cafés (see above) before taking a right turn down Keskuskatu, just before the impressive **Stockmann** department store. At this point, shoppers can head across Mannerheimintie to explore the design and fashion boutiques around Bulevardi, Uudenmaankatu and Erottajankatu – pick up the **Design District Helsinki** map to see the overwhelming choice.

At the end of Keskuskatu is **Railway Square**. To your right, the **Ateneum** (National Gallery) features four caryatids on the front elevation that symbolise painting, sculpture, architecture and graphic art. Crossing the square, the grandiose **Main Railway Station** reflects Finland's National Romantic vision of the early 20th century. What a pity Tallinn was never granted an architectural equivalent. Before the first trains had even rolled, the Russian military moved in during World War I to establish a military hospital and subsequently used the complex as a base during the Finnish Civil War in 1918.

Just east of the station is Mannerheimintie, the main thoroughfare heading northeast away from the city. Look right and you'll notice a strange curved building featuring brushed aluminium and sandblasted glass. This is **Kiasma** (Museum of Contemporary Art), opened in 1999. The project was hugely controversial (a foreign architect was chosen and debate over the visual impact of the building raged), but few would argue that Kiasma hasn't added to Helsinki's appeal. The exhibits may be baffling, but the terrace is glorious. On the opposite side of Mannerheimintie is **Kamppi**, the huge shopping complex and indoor bus terminal that opened in 2006. Go here for high-street shops and fast-food-style cafés.

One of my favourite walks is around **Töölönlahti**, a sea inlet that can be reached by walking a little further north, passing as you go **Finlandia Hall**, probably the most famous work of Alvar Aalto (Finland's celebrated architect and designer) and home to the 2007 camp-fest that is the Eurovision Song Contest. If you want to head around Töölönlahti, go clockwise to pass the **Opera House**. In winter, it's common practice to walk straight across the ice and thus cut out the curves of the path.

Sports fans can press on to the **Olympic Stadium**, originally built in 1938 for the games that never took place in 1940, but which was finally home to the 1952 summer games. Follow the white snorkel of the 72m-high tower, which affords the best views of the city. If time's against you, ride the tram back down Mannerheimintie.

Another option is to cut west after Parliament House down Museokatu, Aurorankatu and Temppelikatu to reach **Temppeliaukio**. This church, hewn from the rock, is one of Helsinki's most popular attractions, and hugely popular with Russians. Whilst interesting, it pales next to the magnificence of the main cathedrals.

From Temppeliaukio, follow **Fredrikinkatu** to bypass the Kamppi centre and head left down Kalevankatu. Turning down Yrjönkatuand you'll be at the foot of Hotel Torni, the tallest building around. This was Helsinki's first skyscraper, and the 12th-floor **Ateljee Bar** is a great place from which to view the city (ladies take note, your bathroom has the best view of all). Smoky and busy with locals, it's worth trying an Urban Mojito, made with lime-twisted gin, mango syrup, soda water, crushed ice and fresh mint. It's not cheap (€8.50), but anyone who's still with me by this stage has definitely earned it.

From the door of Torni, retrace your steps to Kalevankatu, but head directly across until you reach **Bulevardi**, a leafy avenue housing some tasteful galleries and Helsinki's oldest café (Eckberg). Turning left, you emerge once again at Mannerheimintie at the top of Esplanad Park. Mosey back down here to the ferry terminal and a welcome sit down on the way back to Tallinn.

INFORMATION AND MAPS

Helsinki City Tourist & Convention Bureau Pohjoisesplanadi 19; ✆ +358 (0) 9169 3757; www.visithelsinki.fi. First-rate tourist office with helpful staff who can point you towards anything you might want to do (museums, shopping, sauna, island trips, zoo etc), most probably in several different languages simultaneously.

Tour bookings are also arranged here. *Open summer (May–Sep) Mon–Fri 09.00–20.00, Sat–Sun 09.00–18.00. Open winter (Oct–Apr) Mon–Fri 09.00–18.00, Sat–Sun 10.00–16.00.*

Akateeminen Kirjakauppa Keskuskatu 1/Pohjoisesplanadi 39; ☏ +358 (0) 9121 4322; www.visithelsinki.fi. At the top of Pohjoisesplanadi, this is a great place to browse English-language books and newspapers. The excellent third-floor travel department is chock full of maps and guidebooks, including Bradt's very own Helsinki city guide. *Open Mon–Fri 09.00–21.00, Sat 09.00–18.00.*

12 Language

PRONUNCIATION

Words in Estonian are pronounced with the stress on the first syllable. Individual letters are pronounced as follows:

VOWELS

a as the English **u** in **but**
aa is like **a** in **father**
e as in **bet**
ee as in the English **eh**
i as in **pin**
ii as **ee** in **feel**
o as in **off**
oo as **eau** in the French **peau**
u as in **put**
uu as the **oo** in **food**
ä almost as in **cat**, but with a less open mouth
ää is the same as **ä**, but with a more open mouth

ö as **ir** in **girl**, but with rounded lips

öö as the **oeu** in the French **voeu**

õ is peculiar to Estonian and is pronounced with the lips in the position of a short **e** while the tongue is retracted

õõ is the same as **õ**, but longer

ü is produced by pronouncing **i** with a protrusion of the lips and a narrow opening of the mouth

üü is the same as **ü**, but longer and clearer

SIGNS

Parkimine keelatud	No parking
Kiiruspiirang	Speed limit
Sissepääs	Entrance
Mitte siseneda	No entry
Väljapääs	Exit
Tagavaraväljapääs	Emergency exit
Avatud	Open
Suletud	Closed
WC	Toilet

CONSONANTS

b is voiceless, almost like the **p** in **copy**

d is voiceless, as the **t** in **city**

g is voiceless, as the **ck** in **ticket**

k, **p** and **t** are stronger and longer than the voiceless **g**, **b**, and **d**

h is the same as in English, but less aspirated

j like **y** in **you**

l as in **lily**

m is the same as in English, but shorter

n as in English

r is trilled

s is voiceless and weaker than the English **s**

v as in English

z as the **s** in **was**

USEFUL WORDS AND EXPRESSIONS

GREETINGS AND BASIC COMMUNICATION

hello	*tere*
goodbye	*nägemist*
good morning	*tere hommikust*
good evening	*head õhtut*

goodnight	*head ööd*
yes	*jah*
no	*ei*
please	*palun*
thank you	*tänan*
less	*vähem*
a little (more)	*(natuke) rohkem*
enough	*aitab*
now (later)	*praegu (hiljem)*
How long?	*Kui kaua?*
How much (is it)?	*Kui palju (see maksab)?*
When?	*Millal?*
Where (is)?	*Kus (on)?*
Excuse me, please	*Vabandage palun*
Help me, please	*Aidake, palun*
More slowly, please	*Aeglasemalt, palun*
Repeat it, please	*Korrake, palun*
Write it down, please	*Kirjutage see üles, palun*
I do not understand	*Ma ei saa aru*
I do not want	*Ma ei taha*
It is (too) late	*See on (liiga) hilja*
It is bad	*See on halb*

It is good	See on hea
Silence, please	Vaikust palun
Wait	Oodake

TRAVELLING

Call a taxi, please	Kutsuge, palun, takso
Call an ambulance	Kutsuge kiirabi
I have lost my way	Olen eksinud
My car has broken down	Mul läks auto katki
My luggage is missing	Minu pagas on kadunud
passport	pass
valid visa	kehtiv viisa
customs, customs duty	toll, tollimaks
baggage room	pagasiruum
airport	lennujaam
bus stop	bussipeatus
coach terminal	bussijaam
ferry port	reisisadam
railway station	raudteejaam
(city) centre	(kesklinn) keskus
street, square	tänav, väljak
traffic lights	valgusfoor

car repair	*autoparandus*
driver's licence	*juhiluba*
traffic accident	*liiklusõnnetus*
traffic police	*liikluspolitseinik*
back	*tagasi*
forward	*edasi*
straight ahead	*otse*
to the east	*itta*
to the left	*vasakule*
to the north	*põhja*
to the right	*paremale*
to the south	*lõunasse*
to the west	*läände*

MONEY

credit card	*krediitkaart*
currency exchange	*valuutavahetus*
exchange rate	*vahetuskurss*
free of charge	*tasuta*
in cash	*sularahas*

ACCOMMODATION

vacant room	*vaba tuba*
with bath (shower)	*vanniga (dushiga)*
with private toilet	*oma tualettruumiga*
at the front	*tänava poole*
at the back	*hoovi poole*
on a lower floor	*madalamal korrusel*
reduction for children	*allahindlus lastele*
an extra bed	*lisavoodi*
hot and cold water	*soe ja külm vesi*
kitchen facilities	*köögi kasutamine*
Is there a lift?	*Kas teil lift on?*
Please clean this	*Palun see puhastada*
Please wash this	*Palun see pesta*
The voltage is 220	*Elektripinge on 220*

RESTAURANTS AND MEALS

beer	*õlu*
coffee (with milk)	*kohv (piimaga)*
drinking water	*joogivesi*
juice	*mahl*
milk	*piim*

mineral water	*mineraalvesi*
wine (red, white)	*vein (punane, valge)*
wine list	*veinikaart*
Estonian cuisine	*Eesti köök*
beefsteak	*biifsteek*
boiled/oven-baked potatoes	*keedetud/ahjus küpsetatud kartulid*
brown/white bread	*must/valge leib*
fried fish	*praetud kala*
green salad	*roheline salat*
mutton/lamb	*lambaliha/talleliha*
roast chicken	*kanapraad*
roast pork	*seapraad*
roast turkey	*kalkunipraad*
salt	*sool*
seafood	*mereannid*
sugar	*suhkur*
veal	*loomaliha*
vegetable soup	*köögiviljasupp*
vegetarian dishes	*taimetoidud*

DAYS

Monday	*esmaspäev*
Tuesday	*teisipäev*
Wednesday	*kolmapäev*
Thursday	*neljapäev*
Friday	*reede*
Saturday	*laupäev*
Sunday	*puhapäev*
today	*täna*
yesterday	*eile*
tomorrow	*homme*

NUMBERS

1	*üks*	8	*kaheksa*
2	*kaks*	9	*üheksa*
3	*kolm*	10	*kümme*
4	*neli*	11	*üksteist*
5	*viis*	12	*kaksteist*
6	*kuus*	20	*kakskümmend*
7	*seitse*	100	*sada*

13 Further Information

BOOKS

Books published in Tallinn for sale to foreigners, although well produced and well translated, are often disappointing. At one end, they would weigh down even the sturdiest of coffee tables while at the other they are little more than pamphlets. Not much remains in between, apart from some purely photographic souvenirs, and it is surprising that there is still not a single guidebook to Tallinn produced there. Most titles available cover just a single building or a single theme. In this latter category two recent publications stand out, *20th Century Architecture in Tallinn* by Karin Hallas and *Walking in Old Tallinn* by Tõnu Koger. The year 2003 saw the Tallinn Tourist Board beginning to publish for the public. Their first four *Curiosity Walks* pamphlets are titled: *Churches*, *Kadriorg*, *Lower Town* and *Toompea*. Sadly these have not been followed up by others.

The Living Past of Tallinn by Elena Rannu, first published in Soviet times, continues to appear and covers the period up to the death of Peter the Great in 1725. I⁺ effective in its portrayal of day-to-day life on the streets. *The History of Old T'* Raimo Pullat, first published in 1998, is rather ponderous but continues ⁱ⁺ until the beginning of the Soviet era.

The Estonian Institute produces a wide range of fact sheets and two magazines, *Estonian Art* and *ELM (Estonian Literary Magazine)*. Estonian embassies usually stock these but they are now published in full on the institute's website (*www.einst.ee*). They are an excellent substitute for books that still need to be published. In Tallinn they can be obtained from the institute's office at Suur Karja 14. They have a refreshing sense of humour (and sense of realism) lacking in so many other Estonian publications. A second Estonian Institute website (*www.estonica.org*) offers an encyclopaedia of Estonian topics such as culture, history, nature etc.

The secondhand bookshops still have an extensive stock from the Soviet period. These shops also have a good selection of books on art and sculpture, none of which has been subsequently brought up to date. *Tallinn: A Tourist Guidebook* by H Taliste appeared in many editions during the 1970s and 1980s as did *A Guidebook to Tallinn* by Raimo Pullat. Both are interesting not only for the photographs of wide empty streets and statues now pulled down but also for their interpretation of Estonian history. Only ten–12 restaurants were listed throughout this time.

No travel books dating from before World War II have been republished since then but copies of *Baltic Corner: Travel in Estonia* by Ronald Seth, published in 1939, can still be found. Several chapters cover Tallinn. The year 2003 fortunately saw a new edition of Arthur Ransome's *Racundra's First Cruise*, edited by Brian Hammett, which commemorates the 80th anniversary of this expedition which took place in 1923. Not only did Ransome include Tallinn and Paldiski in this journey but he also married his second wife Evgenia at the British Consulate in Tallinn in 1924. She had previously worked as Trotsky's secretary in St Petersburg. The dramatic naval clashes between the British and the Soviet navies that took place a few years earlier close to Tallinn are described in *Freeing the Baltic* by Geoffrey Bennett.

Bradt publish similar guidebooks to this one for Helsinki, Riga and Vilnius. *Estonia: The Bradt Travel Guide* covers a number of places near Tallinn that it was not possible to include here.

MAPS

No decent maps of Tallinn or Estonia are published outside the country. The main publisher in Tallinn is Regio, whose maps are in all the main bookshops. Foreigners planning to travel around Tallinn usually buy their *Ühistranspordi kaart* (public transport map) and those travelling further afield their *Eesti Teede Atlas* (Estonian Road Atlas). These are updated every year and are available in Britain at Stanfords in London, Bristol and Manchester. Maps and atlases covering the three Baltic states are produced by the Latvian publisher Jana Seta and these are available both in Britain and in Estonia.

WEBSITES

Estonian Institute www.einst.ee, www.estonica.org
Estonian Ministry of Foreign Affairs www.vm.ee

Estonian search engine www.neti.ee
Estonian Tourist Board www.visitestonia.com
Tallinn Bus Services www.tak.ee
Tallinn City Council www.tallinn.ee
Tallinn Tourist Board www.tourism.tallinn.ee

WIN £100 CASH!

READER QUESTIONNAIRE

Complete and return this questionnaire for the chance to win £100 cash in our regular draw

(Entries may be posted or faxed to us, or scanned and emailed.)

Your feedback is important. To help us plan future guides please answer all the questions below. All completed questionnaires will qualify for entry in the draw.

Have you used any other Bradt Guides? If so, which titles?. . . . .

. . . .

Where did you buy this guidebook?. . . . .

Your age   16–25 ☐   26–45 ☐   46–60 ☐   60+ ☐

Please send us any comments about this guide or other Bradt Travel Guides. . . . . .

. . . .
. . . .
. . . .

For a current list of titles and prices, please see our website – www.bradtguides.com, or call us for a catalogue.

Order Form

Please send me one copy of the following guide at **half the UK retail price**

Title		Retail price	Half price
....		....	
Post & packing (£1/book UK; £2/book Europe; £3/book rest of world)			....
		Total	....

Name. . . . .

Address . . . .

Tel . . . .   Email . . . .

☐ I enclose a cheque for £ . . . . made payable to Bradt Travel Guides Ltd

☐ I would like to pay by credit card. Number: . . . .

Expiry date . . . . . . / . . . . 3-digit security code (on reverse of card)

☐ Please add my name to your mailing/e-newsletter list. (For Bradt use only.)

☐ I would be happy for you to use my name and comments in Bradt marketing material.

Send your order on this form, with the completed questionnaire, to:

Bradt Travel Guides/TAL
23 High Street, Chalfont St Peter, Bucks SL9 9QE
☏ +44 (0)1753 893444   f +44 (0)1753 892333
e info@bradtguides.com   www.bradtguides.com

Index

accommodation 54–73
Aegna Island 19, 162
airport 49–50
all-night shops 99
Altja 182

Baltic Germans 1, 139
Baltic Times 42
banks 40
bars *see* cafés
bookshops 99–101
budgeting 38
buses and trams, local 49, 51–2
buses, regional 33–4
business 16

cafés and bars x, 85–91
car hire 52
Central Market 103
churches VIII, 20, 43, 150–5
   Alexander Nevsky VIII, 24, 108, 150–5

churches *continued*
   Armenian 118
   Charles's 12–13, 106, **151**
   Dome 24, 26,109, **151**
   Holy Ghost **112,152**, 164
   Niguliste *see* St Nicholas'
   St Michael's 3, 110, **153**
   St Nicholas' 24, 110, **154**
   St Olav's 155
cinemas 94
City Paper 42, 74
Coca–Cola Plaza 94
credit cards 41
Crimean War 8, 138, 174
culture *see* festivals
currency 9, 38, 40–1, 50
cycling 10, 21, 52–3, 177

disabled travellers 36–7
Dominican Monastery 114

economy 11–14
electricity XII
embassies (Estonian) 29
embassies in Tallinn 45–6
Estonia 25, 139
Estonian Art Museum (KUMU) 21, 25, **129–32**, 171
Estonian Institute VI, 14, 204
Estonian language XII, 8–9, 14, **194–202**
Estonian National Theatre 118
European Union 9, 13

ferries 6, 32
festivals 17–18
flights 30–1
food and drink 104–5
Freedom Clock 119
Freedom Square 22, 117, 119
gay Tallinn 97–8
geography 18–19

health 34
helicopter services 31–2
Helsinki 2, 9, 32, **187–93**
history 1–9
hospitals 46
hotels X, 15, 23, **54–73**
House of Blackheads 93

internet centres 44–5
Ilves, Toomas Henrik 11

Kadriorg Palace 3, 21, 25, 134–6,171
Kadriorg Park 156, 171
Käsmu 183–4
Katariina Käik 101–2, 115
Kaubamaja 45, 121
Kolga 186–7
Kross, Jan 110
KUMU *see* Estonian Art Museum

Lahemaa National Park 50, 176–187
language *see* Estonian language
Linnahall 92, 94
Lübeck VII, 154

Mägi, Konrad 131, 185
Manitski, Jaan 185–6
market 103
Meistrite Hoov (Masters' Courtyard) 102
Meri, Lennart 9, 11, 64, 151
Metsakalmistu (Forest Cemetery) 163
money 40–1
museums 21–2, 47–8, **123–49**
  Adamson-Eric 24, **124**
  Applied Arts 125
  Architecture 125–6

museums *continued*
  City 24, 114, **126–7**
  Dolls 127–8
  Eduard Vilde 128
  Energy 128
  Estonian Art Museum (KUMU) 21, 25, **129–32**
  Estonian Bank 119, **126**
  Estonian History **112**, **132–3**
  Fire-Fighting 133
  Foreign Art *see* Kadriorg Palace
  Health 134
  Kalev Chocolate 136–7
  Kiek in de Kök 108, **138**
  KUMU *see* Estonian Art Museum
  Laidoner 163–4
  Maarjamäe 167–8
  Marine Mine 113–14
  Maritime 24–5, 113, **139**
  Mikkel 25, **139–40**, 171–2
  Natural History 142
  National Library 106, 118, **140–2**
  Occupation 106, 142–3
  Photographic 111, **145**
  Rocca al Mare 21, **146–8**
  Theatre and Music 136

Naissaar Island 19, **173–6**
National Library *see* museums

NATO 12
nightlife 92, **94–6**
Northern War VIII

Olympic Games (1980) 9, 162, 165
Open-air museum *see* Rocca al Mare
opera 93

Paldiski 53, 159–61
Palmse Manor 178–81
Parliament 108, 144
Päts, Konstantin 135–6, 169
Peter The Great VIII, 3, 7, 119, 134, 136, 144, 167
pharmacies 46, 112, 144
Pikk Hermann 107
Pirita 162–5
population XII
port 6, 32, 49, 62
post cards 99–101
post offices 44
public holidays XII, 18
public transport 47–8, 51–2

religion XII, 16–17, 46
restaurants X, XII, 39, 74–84
Rocca al Mare 21, 53, 157–9
Rüütel, Arnold 10, 11

safety 35
Sagadi 181–2
Sakala Conference Centre 119
Savissaar, Edgar 10
school holidays XII
shopping 99–104
Smull, Juhan 110
Song Festival Grounds 25,170,
souvenirs 101–4
Soviet Union (USSR) 4–5, 6–7, 8–9, 10–12, 28,
130, 137,141, 154, 160,166–7,169,170, 171,
176, 204
Soviet War Memorial 166–7
supermarkets 103–4
synagogue 121

Tall Herman Tower see Pikk Hermann
Tallinn In Your Pocket 42, 43, 56, 74, 95
Tallinn Card 47–8, 52, 123
Tallinn Tourist Board VI, 18, 47
taxis 49, 50–1
telephones 42–4
tipping 39
Toompea Hill VIII, 21, 24
tour operators 26–8, 47
   American 28
   British 26–7

tour operators *continued*
   Canadian 28
   Estonian 47
Tourist Information Centre 47, 110
Town Hall Square 3, 23, 111–2
trains 34
trams and buses 51–2
travellers' cheques 41
TV Tower 166–7

USSR *see* Soviet Union

Viinistu 185–6
Vilde, Eduard 110, 172
Viru Gate 115,118
visas 28–9
Võsu 183

walking tours 106–122
Wall of Sweaters 102, 115
weather XII, 19–20
websites XI, 205–6
Wiiralt, Eduard 185
wine 75, 86
World War I 5–8
World War II 5–8,110–11,141, 142–3

I TALLINN

Bay of Tallinn

0 ——— 400m
0 ——— 400yds

I
Patarei Prison
Linnahall
Heliport
Harbour Terminals A, B & C
Tourist information
Portus
Harbour Terminal D
Maarjamäe Palace
Viimsi
Exhibition Centre
Narva
PIRITA TEE
SADAMA

2
Railway station
Architecture Museum
SADAMA
Song Festival Amphitheatre
Rüssalka Memorial
NARVA MNT
OLD TOWN (VANALINN)
PIKK
MERE PST
AHTRI
Coca-Cola Plaza
Forum
Central
Central post office
see page 2 for Old Town
KADRIORG
Kadriorg Park
Kadriorg Palace
WEIZENBERGI
Peter the Great Museum
Park Museum
LAASNAMAE TEE
Narva

3
Keila, Paldiski
PÄRNU MNT
VIRU
ESTONIA PST
Viru
Tallink
GONSIORI
SAS Radisson
TARTU MNT
St John's Almshouses
RAVALA PST
A. LAUTERI
PRONKSI
RAUA
JOE
NARVA MNT
Park
GONSIORI
VILMSI
POSKA
Mikkel Museum
KUMU (Estonian Art Museum)
Kadriorg Stadium
LAAGNA TEE
LAAGNA TEE
N
Bradt
PAE
Narva
PUNANE

4
Olümpia
LIIVALAIA
LIIVALAIA
Keila, Paldiski
VEERENNI
Central market
JUHKENTALI
Kalevi Stadium
Siselinni Cemetery
Sõjaväe Cemetery
© Bradt Travel Guides Ltd
Bus station
TARTU MNT
LASNAMÄE
PALLASTI
MAJAKA
PAE
PETERBURI TEE
Susi
Ülemiste Station
Lake Ülemiste
Airport, Tartu
Ülemiste
SUUR - SÕJAMÄE
LASNAMÄE
Narva

A   B   C   D   E

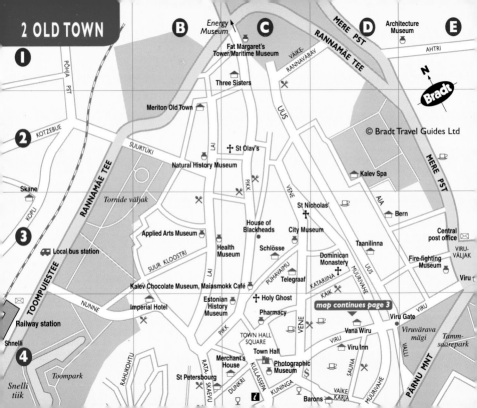